6   Report

The Church and Social Cohesion
Connecting Communities and Serving People

Madeleine Pennington

Praise for *The Church and Social Cohesion*

Too often in studies of community cohesion the place of religion is treated either as only a problem to be solved or as an irrelevance to be ignored. This excellent report brings home the power and potential for the Church at the heart of our communities and provokes us to think what more we might do together in the future.

The Most Reverend and Right Honourable Justin Welby
Archbishop of Canterbury

This report sheds light on how Churches across the nation have been instrumental in banding our communities together through a tumultuous and challenging year, unparalleled in living history. It is a powerful testimony to how the Church, across the breadth of its expression, has been working publicly and behind the scenes to serve its people and foster positive social cohesion to keep the nation unified.

H E Archbishop Angaelos, OBE
Coptic Orthodox Archbishop of London
Orthodox President, Churches Together in England

This report on 'The Church and Social Cohesion' prepared by the Free Churches Group, in partnership with Theos, is a welcome resource as we deal with issues that have the potential to fragment and divide our society. At a time when we, as a nation, are dealing with the complex, emotional and often painful issues that have arisen as a result of Brexit, Black Lives Matter and the COVID-19 pandemic amongst others, the Church has a critical role to play in bringing about unity in communities. This report will not only encourage churches to play that role but will also help other stakeholders to understand the importance of the Church in our communities.

Pastor Agu Irukwu
Pentecostal President, Churches Together in England
National Leader of The Redeemed Christian Church of God

For centuries, churches across England have played a key role in the glue that holds local communities together. This remains true today, a time when people are more likely to encounter their local church through its community services than its worship services. Maddy Pennington's report is unusual for the richness of its insights into the contributions of local churches to social cohesion, from both the perspective of church participants and the wider community. As the report shows, churches are much more than buildings – they are an indispensable part of our social fabric. Every day they are actively building networks, forming leaders, bringing people together across the lines of division, mobilising volunteers, convening a wide range of actors and amplifying positive, shared visions for the future.

Tim Dixon
Co-founder, More in Common

The Christian Church in England, of all denominations, is arguably the single most cohesive force in our society. No other institution has its national breadth, its local depth or the diversity of its activity. This research provides vital evidence of the strength of the Church today and its role in building better connected, more unified communities.

Danny Kruger MP
MP for Devizes

Churches around the country are knitting the bonds within community, working alongside others for love, justice and peace. This timely report reminds us of what churches have to offer to building flourishing communities, as we seek to be part of God's Kingdom.

Rachel Lampard MBE
Past Vice-President of the Methodist Conference
Team Leader of the Joint Public Issues Team

From time to time the Christian community stops just long enough to go beyond its internal pre-occupations and evaluate its contribution to the community we are called to serve. This report is a bold attempt to explore how far the church's actions speak even louder than its words.

Reverend Dr Joel Edwards CBE
Former Director General, Evangelical Alliance UK
International Director, Micah Challenge
Church Leader within the Assemblies of God

I am delighted to endorse this report which comes at a critical time for the church and the country as the importance of social cohesion is brought into sharp relief by both the Covid-19 pandemic and the Black Lives Matter movement. The recommendations in the report provide clear and compelling advice to the church as it seeks to bring the presence of Jesus into communities through acts of love and service.

Simon Blanchflower CBE
Chief Executive Officer of East West Rail
Church leader at Latymer Community Church,
Ladbroke Grove, London

It has been a pleasure to serve as an observer on the Advisory Group to the Commission. The Report draws attention to the importance of social cohesion in England during difficult and fractious times. From a Caritas perspective I welcome the focus on building a society in which everyone feels they have a stake, and all are enabled to contribute to the common good.

Dr Philip McCarthy
Chief Executive Officer, Caritas Social Action Network

Contents

Contents

Advisory Group to the Commission 6

Acknowledgements 9

Foreword 13

Executive Summary 17

Introduction 29

1. From crisis to community: the Church and social
   cohesion policy 38

   A crisis-driven approach: faith as a risk factor 39
   Taking a wider perspective: the churches as a community
      resource 45
   From crisis to community: loving your neighbour as a Christian
      imperative 49
   Theological reflections: social cohesion in the churches' own
      words 51
   Conclusion 55

2. Church assets 61

   Buildings: churches as places of gathering 63
   Networks: churches as the "capillaries" of community 74
   Leadership: churches representing and empowering the
      community 87
   Convening power: churches as trusted facilitators 95
   Volunteers: churches as congregations in action 98
   Vision: "I felt God asking me a question" 102
   Conclusion 108

3. The Church and other organisations 117

   Interfaith engagement 118
   Ecumenical networks 123
   Council-church relationships 126
   Conclusion 135

Conclusion and Recommendations 139

Appendix: Case Study Areas 147

Advisory Group to the Commission

The Commission was set up in mid-2018 with five advisors who have a Free Church background:

Rachel Lampard	Past Vice-President of the Methodist Conference and Team Leader of the Joint Public Issues Team (comprising the Methodist Church, the Baptist Union of Great Britain, the United Reformed Church and the Church of Scotland).
Jennifer Laurent-Smart	Equality and Diversity Manager for the Salvation Army.
Andrew Bradstock	Professor Emeritus in the Department of Theology, Religion and Philosophy at the University of Winchester; former Secretary for Church and Society with the United Reformed Church and member of the Joint Public Issues Team.
Joel Edwards	Former General Director of the Evangelical Alliance UK; International Director, Micah Challenge; and church leader within the Assemblies of God.
Trevor Howard	Executive Vice-Chair of Churches in Communities International; member of the Free Churches Board.

And five observers nominated by the other Churches Together in England Presidents (as they were in 2018):

Martin Kettle (2018-19) Nominated on behalf of the Archbishop of Canterbury.

Ben Ryan (2020)

Philip McCarthy Nominated on behalf of the Cardinal Archbishop of Westminster.

Simon Blanchflower Nominated by Billy Kennedy (then President of the 4th Presidency Group).

Fr Kyrillos Asaad Nominated by the Coptic Orthodox Archbishop of London.

R. David Muir Nominated on behalf of Pastor Agu Irukwu, the Pentecostal President.

The Commission received administrative support and guidance from:

Paul Rochester The General Secretary of the Free Churches Group.

Paul Gutteridge Public Affairs Advisor to the Free Churches Group.

Author's Acknowledgements

I would like to thank colleagues at Theos for their support in the production of this report: particular thanks are due to Elizabeth Oldfield, Nick Spencer, Paul Bickley, Hannah Rich and Simon Perfect for feedback on earlier drafts; to Ben Ryan, Laura Moulton, Simeon Burke and Hannah Eves for heroic efforts in gathering data across the case study areas; and to Simon Perfect and Mehr Panjwani for assisting in the final data analysis. Thank you also to Emily Downe, Lizzie Stanley, Polly Parrott, Rebekah Davison, Debbie Clifford and the publishing team at the Bible Society for their work on the design and publication of the report – and to Peter Brierley for sharing his own research with me in the later stages of this project. I am also extremely grateful to the Advisory Group to the Commission, and the additional input of Hugh Osgood, Paul Rochester and Paul Gutteridge as a Steering Group, whose insight and advice has been invaluable at every stage of the process. Of course, this research was made what it is by the participants themselves: I thank them for their time, wisdom, experience and critical voice, and hope they see their communities reflected in what I have written. Finally, special thanks go to the funders of this project – the Westhill Trust and the Free Churches Group itself – whose support for the work, and passion to see a more cohesive society, has made this Commission possible.

Free Churches Group
Acknowledgements

The Free Churches Group acknowledges the grant from Westhill Trust towards the first year of research on this project.

Foreword

This report was commissioned by the Free Churches Group to provide an objective assessment of the contribution of the Church to social cohesion at a local level across England. It was decided from the outset that the understanding of "the Church" would not be limited to Free Churches, but would reflect the breadth of churches present in each community studied. It was also agreed that the specific elements contributing to social cohesion would not be tightly defined in advance but allow scope for the studies to cover specific local situations in respect of social cohesion. Having said this, a great deal of thought went into establishing a list of geographically and sociologically diverse local communities.

Those familiar with the Free Churches Group will know that we bring together a wide range of denominations, representing 28% of all church congregations in England and Wales. Our members include the Methodist Church, the Baptist Union of Great Britain, the United Reformed Church and the Salvation Army, as well as many Pentecostal groupings and other significant denominations with national spread that have a strong Free Church tradition. In effect, we offer a gathering point for most Trinitarian churches that are not within the Church of England, the Roman Catholic Church and the Orthodox Churches.

Within the public arena, Free Churches are best known for our work in health care, the prison service and education, where we not only provide informed input at a policy level but supply Free Church Chaplains to serve in the nation's hospitals, prisons, schools, colleges and universities, and increasingly in other areas too. It is our privilege to speak out at a national level, often with the Anglicans, Catholic, and Orthodox and others within Churches Together in England, and it is with this sense of working together that we have commissioned this report.

The report is not, therefore, a promotion of the work of the Free Churches, but rather a critical analysis of all churches regarding social cohesion today. We could have commissioned research that made a feature of our work on social cohesion through hospitals, prisons and education at a national level. However, we preferred to commission a report of the work of all churches operating at a local level, and to reflect the balance of issues and perceptions of performance that local communities have raised and provided.

To my mind this is an incredibly important and timely report, and will become all the more so as COVID-19 restrictions are lifted. The Church is no longer presuming on an entitlement in public life, but demonstrating its value in tangible ways throughout local communities based on its ministry and mission as followers of Jesus who came to serve rather than to be served. Although we have a history of doing this in different ways in different centuries and throughout many decades, we are still evaluating and adapting to need; and it seems that we are again gaining recognition and appreciation for our initiative-taking and contributions.

I acknowledge the support and guidance given by the Advisory Group and with them express a sincere debt of gratitude to the research team from Theos led by Dr Madeleine Pennington who worked so hard on our behalf to carry out the research and write the report.

Hugh Osgood
Free Churches Moderator
Free Churches President of Churches Together in England
Chair of the Free Churches Commission on the Church and Social Cohesion

Executive Summary

What do Brexit, Black Lives Matter, loneliness, and austerity have in common? They are all social cohesion issues. At heart, social cohesion is about which communities we feel part of – locally, nationally, internationally, and even virtually – and how coherently these communities interrelate. It is about how connected and accountable we feel to others across society, and how fairly opportunities are distributed. It is about whether, and to what extent, we feel we belong. Simply, it is about how effectively we nurture what is most precious to us: the strength of our collective relationships.

Social cohesion affects every aspect of our lives from happiness to economic flourishing. It has been towards the top of the policy agenda for several decades, over which time British society has become more culturally and ethnically diverse, older, less equal, and more geographically mobile. These shifts do not inherently undermine social cohesion, but they do mean we are less likely to have common experiences with our neighbours by default – and unfortunately, our interactions with those in our communities have not kept pace with the changing nature of society. Time and effort are required to bring people together and nourish cohesive communities, and there is work to do.

The nation's churches have the potential to offer this time and effort in abundance, but neither the churches' community contribution nor its wider potential have been considered in detail by policymakers. Therefore, the Free Churches Group commissioned Theos to assess the impact of churches on social cohesion in October 2018.

Between November 2018 and September 2019, Theos conducted 361 semi-structured interviews with individuals across fourteen local authorities within England, as well as observing a range of local cohesion initiatives in each of the case study areas. The areas we visited were: Bolton, Bradford, Bury, Cornwall, Croydon, Derby, East Lindsey, Haringey, Middlesbrough, Newham, Peterborough, Plymouth, Solihull, and Thanet.

The findings of the Commission are organised into three chapters:

Chapter One: From crisis to community: the Church and social cohesion policy

Chapter one briefly summarises how policy interventions in pursuit of greater social cohesion have usually been driven forward by crisis, and therefore predominantly focus on what happens when things have already gone wrong. Because of this policy approach, faith and belief groups in general are understood primarily as a risk factor for division; churches in particular are viewed as a lever to be pulled in an emergency, or, at worst, as a problem to be solved.

Nonetheless, when we take a wider view of cohesion as something that affects all of us (whether in crisis or not) we find that churches are often working quietly and concertedly to enhance their communities. Previous research has found that people with a religious affiliation are more active citizens than those without, and that frequently practising Christians (defined by regular prayer and church attendance) are the most likely religious grouping in London to join a political party, make a charitable donation, or volunteer regularly for a local charitable initiative. The increased role of Christians following public spending cuts in an age of austerity has been particularly striking. Churches are embedded in their communities, working behind the scenes and below the radar – and indeed, their community engagement works best on precisely this basis (that is, listening to what communities need, tailoring responses to local circumstances, and prioritising what the community and congregation will support on a sustainable basis).

Moreover, when participants have told us about their motivations for civic and community engagement, we have found they do so for authentically Christian reasons, as an outworking of their faith convictions. Many of our participants offered theologically-grounded reflections on their engagement with the community; particularly common themes were the need to follow Christ's example, the call to be "salt and light" in the community, bringing the marginalised into the centre, building the "Kingdom of God", and love of neighbour.

Chapter Two: Church assets

Considering the particularities of churches' community engagement in more detail, and inspired by the insights of asset-based community development, six common church-based assets came up again and again:

Buildings: It is important to note that, while churches have continued to provide basic community services through the COVID-19 pandemic, their broader capacity to encourage serendipitous or casual in-person meeting through their buildings is almost entirely restricted by current regulations. However, before the pandemic, church buildings were used as vital gathering points for community activity, offered cheaply or for free, and (unlike many statutory services) scattered equally throughout our communities rather than being concentrated only in busy metropolitan centres. The cohesion impact of this physical space is particularly marked given the dramatic decline in other forms of community space over recent years. Churches can become community hubs and local landmarks which encourage positive feelings of solidarity in their neighbourhoods; they are places of hope and welcome for many of the most vulnerable in society. At the same time, buildings can also be experienced as a distraction or a burden by church congregations themselves, leading to unfulfilled potential in other areas where community engagement is concerned – even as churches which do not have their own buildings also face additional cohesion challenges, including greater suspicion from outside parties.

Networks: Deep and wide community networks build up around churches at the "capillary" level of our communities. This can be through worship (in which the bonding of people around a shared faith enables bridging opportunities along other forms of difference) or through the many community events which are run through and by churches. These networks are invaluable as a direct antidote to social isolation and loneliness, to amplify community responses, and to cascade information quickly and effectively throughout communities. One aspect of the churches' community profile which is sometimes viewed less positively, as a negative form of network-building, is the presence of church-run schools. Church-run schools should work within their communities and alongside the relevant authorities to make their admissions policies as inclusive as possible. However, their existence is not itself inherently damaging to cohesive societies, and the wider debate around schools with a religious character can cause tensions that have a negative cohesion impact of their own.

Leadership: Churches are wellsprings of formal and informal community leadership, forming (and paying) community champions who take initiative and empower their neighbourhoods, building up "dignity" and a sense of "purpose" in individuals and groups. Most obviously, visible and public faith leadership at a formal level can be extremely helpful in times of crisis – but beyond this, church leadership in the community is most effectively released where the natural skills and passions of ordinary Christians are nurtured through church, rather than relying solely on ordained church leaders to act within the community. At its best, this happens from a young age, although youth ministry (and particularly within that, a unified voice on the issue of youth violence) is a significant area in which churches could be working more concertedly and connectedly together.

Volunteers: Volunteering activity is a proxy measure for social cohesion in its own right, and churches generate significant volunteering efforts among practising Christians. This contribution is not always focused on Christian-run activities, but the churches do also play an important role in coordinating volunteers where activity is church-based.

Convening power: We found several striking instances where churches and church leaders were acting as trusted facilitators, convening the community in times of challenge or celebration. This is certainly bolstered by the cultural significance of the establishment of the Church of England, though convening power does emerge naturally (and just as effectively) across all church and faith traditions.

Vision: A vision for change and transformation is perhaps the most important – certainly the most unifying – of the churches' cohesion assets. Community initiatives work best where there is a vision driving them forward, and this often emerges naturally from the spiritual lives of Christians who feel led by God to serve their communities. Those outside the Church should not be threatened by this, but rather see it as a gift to (and a strength of) the community. At the same time, some aspects of some churches' vision can also be divisive. The main issue here is some churches' teaching on issues around sexuality and gender; however, while this is an important issue in its own right, it was mentioned less than might be expected in the specific context of the churches' impact on social cohesion.

Chapter Three: the Church and other organisations

Finally, chapter three evaluates how effectively churches work with other organisations in the pursuit of social cohesion goals, through three case studies:

Interfaith work: Interfaith engagement can happen organically, where pre-existing faith and church structures act as the conduit for acts of solidarity and expressions of intention to move towards a more cohesive and peaceful future. More often, formal interfaith work is the most active and sustained channel for communication between faiths. It is a common criticism that this sort of interfaith work tends to involve those who are already convinced of its value, with little wider participation. Certainly, enthusiasm for interfaith work differs hugely between churches (and even within congregations), and there is significant scope for expansion; many participants also indicated that there was a need to move beyond conversation, and that task-based engagement was the most effective way to involve whole communities (rather than just official leaders) in forging links between faith and belief groups. Nonetheless, even these efforts often rely on sustained communication behind the scenes, and although it is always positive to see wider participation in interfaith engagement, the interfaith work which is already happening remains extremely valuable for nurturing strategic community relationships; it is under-appreciated and would be noticed if it disappeared.

Ecumenical engagement: Churches themselves are by no means all the same, and the variety within Christianity can foster a unique cohesion dynamic by which otherwise distinct communities feel a natural sense of collegiality with one another. This is a striking way in which bonding capital (around a shared Christian identity) can strengthen bridging opportunities (around ethnicity, socio-economic status, age, and culture). Ecumenical links can also help non-Christian groups engage with churches through a single point of contact, and the impact of practical church responses in the community is often greater where churches work together. However, such working relationships are not always straightforward: ecumenical forums can end up gravitating towards particular ecclesiastical traditions, and with an increasingly dynamic church landscape (particularly in urban areas) it requires a concerted effort (and even paid time) to involve everybody.

Church-council relationships: In an age of austerity, local authorities have necessarily strengthened their engagement with churches as they take on a greater role in the provision of services. However, churches are less often included in conversations and initiatives specifically pertaining to cohesion issues, and this can be a missed opportunity. Not everybody welcomes the churches' role in service delivery; concerns largely pertain to fears around proselytism and the exemptions which religious groups enjoy from the Equality Act 2010. However, there is legal provision to prevent inappropriate discrimination when religious groups are acting on behalf of a public authority, and the vast majority of churches have reflected carefully and thoughtfully on the relationship between evangelism and the responsibility to provide safe and accessible services. That said, churches themselves can also feel uncomfortable about expectations placed on them to provide services, and the perception that they are wasting resources if they do not direct them entirely towards the wider community: while they act out of their religious motivation to serve their communities, they are not just service providers in a secular sense, and their relationships with secular authorities (and society as a whole) work best where the distinctive assets of all parties are recognised and celebrated on their own terms.

Conclusion and Recommendations

From this discussion, the report draws three major conclusions, out of which recommendations for both churches and policymakers emerge.

First, at their best and in contrast to much of cohesion policy which has been driven forward in crisis, churches are emblematic of an approach that views cohesion as a desirable outcome in its own right. They are embedded in their local communities and often working concertedly under the radar to bolster the strength of our collective relationships. Therefore, policymakers should ensure that they are working with churches wherever possible and appropriate, as a practical step towards a less crisis-driven approach to cohesion.

For their own part, churches most successfully serve their neighbourhoods where they capitalise on this natural strength – so where churches themselves want to start something new, they should first consider what is already going on in the neighbourhood, what the community needs, and what the congregation will support. In other words, their engagement should be tailored to the community in which the church sits.

At the same time, where they have a realistic understanding of their own resources, their impact on social cohesion can be thoroughly transformative; therefore, alongside a recognition of community need, churches should take time systematically to reflect on their available assets, and consider ways in which existing resources can be used more effectively.

In this sense, the Commission recognises the insights of both needs-based and asset-based community development. Are "bump moments" between rental groups being maximised? Are rental prices affordable for local and grassroots or charity groups? Do congregations feel empowered to take on leadership roles? Are maintenance concerns a distraction or a burden? What can be done to release the natural assets of the church into service, and make churches more accessible to individuals in the community?

Secondly, on many of these points, churches illustrate the limitations of any approach that views only bridging capital as a route to a more cohesive society. There many instances where bonding capital along one measure can generate bridging capital along a range of others; so too, bonding capital itself can be highly positive as a way of promoting feelings of belonging and confidence, and indeed, of enabling a range of people from different backgrounds to feel equal ownership over the public sphere. A truly cohesive society is not one in which everybody agrees, but one in which everyone feels they have a stake – and this equally requires bridging and bonding opportunities. In this sense, this report has offered a practical elaboration on the conceptual conclusions of the *Cohesive Societies: Faith and Belief* review published earlier this year: those working on cohesion issues should be prepared to engage with, and promote, both bridging and bonding opportunities as they emerge practically in local communities and beyond. Working with churches is one concrete way in which they can do this.

That said, there is a clear difference between promoting positive bonding capital and bolstering existing inequalities, or entrenching inward-looking communities. Throughout churches' congregational life, but especially where they have a clearly delineated responsibility to serve the wider community (for example, through church-run schools or the provision of council-funded community services) they should take special care to promote inclusion and diversity in their spaces; this includes mitigating against any negative impact of faith-based school admissions on existing inequalities.

Thirdly, churches are not just generic community groups, and their full potential is realised only where the distinctive features that come with their Christian motivation are recognised. Not only do churches have their own authentic motivations for engaging in the community (chapter one), and a particular pattern of assets which characterises their nature as churches (chapter two), but the way they engage with others is marked by their authentic nature as churches (chapter three). What makes positive interfaith engagement is not necessarily the same as what makes positive ecumenical work, or a positive relationship between church and council. There is room for all these relationships in a truly cohesive society, in all their diversity and specificity – and cohesion is served best when each party is recognised for what it can uniquely offer. Therefore, those working on cohesion policy and strategy – whether local authorities, charities, police, healthcare professionals, other faith groups, or even churches themselves – should take account of the specific ways in which churches operate in their communities, and include them at the decision-making table on this basis rather than expecting everyone to engage in the same way.

A local church can be an economic and relational lifeline to individuals and groups; it can be an effective convenor of local stakeholder relationships, and a powerhouse of both paid and unpaid time; it can raise passionate leaders from within the community, who have the networks to understand what is really going on, and the vision to see potential where others do not. A society which embraces the role of churches as key stakeholders in cohesion discussions on this basis will be a more rounded one, more comfortable with difference, and more confident in its underlying unity. That is to say, it will be more cohesive – both at a local level and beyond.

Recommendations in brief:

Policymakers should...

(1) Ensure that they are working with churches wherever possible and appropriate as part of a move away from a crisis-driven approach;

(2) Be prepared to engage with, and promote, both bridging and bonding opportunities as they emerge practically in local communities and beyond;

(3) Take account of the specific ways in which churches operate in their communities.

Churches should...

(4) Build on the natural strength of their embeddedness in community to tailor their engagement to the community in which they sit, what the community needs, and what their congregation will support;

(5) Systematically reflect on their assets to ensure they are being used to their maximum potential in pursuit of better social cohesion outcomes;

(6) If involved in providing services for the whole community, such as public service delivery or education, ensure inclusion and diversity are promoted in their spaces.

For further practical suggestions for how churches and policymakers can engage and work effectively together on cohesion issues, see the 'How To' booklets published alongside this report. They are entitled *Nurturing Social Cohesion: Why it matters and what your church can do about it* and *Nurturing Social Cohesion: A how-to guide for engaging churches*. They can be downloaded from the Theos website, or requested from the Free Churches Group.

Introduction

What do Brexit, Black Lives Matter, loneliness, and austerity have in common? They are all social cohesion issues. At heart, social cohesion is about which communities we feel part of – locally, nationally, internationally, and even virtually – and how coherently these communities interrelate. It is about how connected and accountable we feel to others across society, and how fairly opportunities are distributed. It is about whether, and to what extent, we feel we belong. Simply, it is about how effectively we nurture what is most precious to us: the strength of our collective relationships.

Social cohesion affects every aspect of our lives, from happiness to economic flourishing, and has been towards the top of the policy agenda for several decades.[1] Over this period, British society has become more culturally and ethnically diverse, older, less equal, and more geographically mobile. These shifts do not inherently undermine social cohesion, but they do mean we are less likely to have common experiences with our neighbours by default. And indeed, our interactions with those in our communities have unfortunately not kept pace with the changing nature of society: we are less integrated by social grade, age, and ethnicity than we would be if there were no social segregation at all.[2] Time and effort are required to bring people together and nourish cohesive communities, and there is work to do.

The nation's churches offer this time and effort in abundance. Across the UK, over 45,000 church congregations (including over 36,000 in England alone) are spread throughout our villages, towns, and cities – and they are a vital part of the social fabric.[3] A local church can be an economic and relational lifeline to individuals and groups; it can be an effective convenor of local stakeholder relationships, and a powerhouse of both paid and unpaid time; it can raise passionate leaders from within the community, who have the networks to understand what is really going on, and the vision to see potential where others do not.

However, cohesion policy has often neglected this contribution and its wider potential, having focused instead on what happens when things go wrong. Churches are viewed as at best a lever to be pulled in an emergency – at worst, as a problem to be solved.[4]

For this reason, the Free Churches Group commissioned Theos to assess the impact of churches on social cohesion in October 2018. The aims of this Commission are to establish what churches are already doing at the local level to help or hinder social cohesion, how this relates to their religious concerns, and what features of the church contribution are important in moving communities towards or away from cohesion.

Between November 2018 and September 2019, Theos conducted semi-structured interviews across fourteen local authorities within England: Bolton, Bradford, Bury, Cornwall, Croydon, Derby, East Lindsey, Haringey, Middlesbrough, Newham, Peterborough, Plymouth, Solihull, and Thanet. These areas enabled us to consider a range of potential cohesion challenges in both rural and urban contexts, and a brief profile of each is offered in Appendix 1. The research was limited to England for comparison, but all nine administrative regions of England were represented.[5] In addition, researchers spoke to a small sample of subject-matter experts, and participants in Pentecostal and charismatic church traditions which were otherwise under-represented in the initial sample.

In total, Theos researchers conducted interviews with 361 participants across England, and observed a range of local cohesion initiatives in each of the case study areas. Of all participants, only 42% spoke on behalf of a church community (for example, church leaders, chaplains, and church-based volunteers) and the remainder were local and national stakeholders speaking in a non-church capacity (for example, council officers, police and healthcare professionals, elected representatives, and other faith leaders). Within the church sample, a range of ecclesiastical traditions were represented: just over half of church-based participants represented a "Free", Nonconformist or Orthodox (as opposed to Catholic or Anglican) ecclesiastical tradition.

The data were collected before the UK's official departure from the EU in January 2020, and before the COVID-19 pandemic, though Brexit negotiations were ongoing throughout the investigation. Where appropriate, we have reflected on how later events may have impacted the Church's community engagement – and indeed, how it may affect this engagement in the future. However, this is not a study of how churches have responded to Brexit or the pandemic. The social, political, and cultural landscape in which churches operate is constantly shifting, but it is hoped that the report's findings have a resonance which transcends these specific (albeit historic) conditions.

Indeed, the need to move beyond a narrow crisis-driven approach is a central principle of the report, as chapter one will unpack in a brief summary of the policy landscape into which this research is offered. Chapter two will then explore the ways in which the churches' distinctive assets positively or negatively affect cohesion, and how effectively they are currently being mobilised. Social cohesion requires working together with others who are different from ourselves – as does fulfilling one's potential to enact positive change in the community – and chapter three will assess the health of such critical working relationships between churches and non-Christian organisations in the pursuit of cohesion goals. Finally, the conclusion will offer practical recommendations for churches and secular organisations alike in the common pursuit of more cohesive communities.

As indicated by the high proportion of non-church participants, this report was not commissioned to praise the church contribution wholesale, nor to shy away from the hard questions. It will outline various areas where church potential could be better fulfilled – and indeed, where churches might actively damage social cohesion, both locally and nationally. Nonetheless, it does seek to correct a neglect of churches' role in policy discussions, moving the conversation away from a focus on risk and crisis, towards resourcefulness, fruitful collaboration, and love of neighbour.

'The strength of our collective relationships': a brief definitional note on social cohesion

Definitions of social cohesion are notoriously contested – and the term is regularly used interchangeably with community cohesion, integration and assimilation, although all have different emphases. "Community cohesion" was the preferred term of policy-makers in the early 2000s, and usually refers to relationships between distinct groups ('communities') of people – sometimes, though not always, in contrast to the structural issues affecting society as a whole.[6] The government's own definition of "community cohesion" in 2007 was presented as a list of characteristics of a society in which "different groups of people... get on well together".[7] More recently, policy has tended to favour terminology of "integration", which refers to mixing between different individuals or groups – for example, different ages, socio-economic groups or ethnicities.[8] One distinctive form of integration which many view as undesirable is "assimilation", since it has connotations of the erasure of difference and the pursuit of 'sameness' across society.[9] None of these terms are limited in scope to a concern for minority-majority ethnic relations, but (as we shall see in chapter one) this has often been the focus in cohesion policy in practice.

Social cohesion itself is often presented as a tick-list of various economic, social, structural and even environmental criteria for community success. It may include any of these things, or not. However, what we might think of intuitively as good cohesion outcomes are not guaranteed by any of them. By way of an example, East Lindsey performs badly on almost every economic and educational metric, yet scores above the national average on sense of belonging, strength of social relationships, and satisfaction with the local area as a place to live.[10] As noted in a recent Onward report, "community is both imagined – a complex and interrelated web of feelings, relationships and personal commitments – and real – the places, institutions and activities that substantiate our sense of belonging".[11] With this "imagined" element in mind, we asked our participants what *they* understood by the term "social cohesion", and various participants expressed doubt over its exact meaning, or reflected that it was not language they would ever use. It was also recognised that its hallmarks might change from place to place:

> *I would say this: first of all, there is a whole lot of difference between social cohesion here [in East Lindsey], and social cohesion for when I used to live in Islington. So they are two completely different things, you know, but the same word.*[12]

So there is no neutral definition of a cohesive society: we are dealing with a contested term, difficult to measure, and perhaps impossible to replicate across communities with fundamentally differing circumstances. Nonetheless, common themes did emerge across our participants' responses – most notably, collaboration to face shared challenges together, tolerance towards others, acceptance of difference, and solidarity and respect between groups. These themes point to something broader than integration alone, albeit retaining a focus on how we deal with those outside our immediate 'in-groups'. For this reason, we have understood social cohesion simply to refer to the strength of our collective relationships – that is, what binds us together beyond our immediate social circles, whether in times of celebration or challenge. In more concrete terms, how far do you feel your own wellbeing is tied to the wellbeing of a person you have never spoken to, but who is sat next to you on the bus?

Consequently, this report is concerned with the general social health of the communities we visited – and whether churches are making a difference. We might conceive of success maturing broadly from mere toleration of difference, to active cooperation, and eventually to genuine relationship; failure might resemble either conflict or apathy towards the community. To this end, we have not judged the success of the churches visited by whether their communities (many of which were facing formidable cohesion challenges) were consistently cohesive. Rather, we considered whether they were helping to move their communities along this scale in a positive direction; after all, moving from apathy to tolerance may be as significant a shift in one area as a move from cooperation to relationship elsewhere.

[1] See, for example, J. Delhey, 'Happier Together. Social cohesion and subjective well-being in Europe', *International Journal of Psychology* 51:3 (2015), p. 163-176; Social Integration Commission, *Social integration: a wake-up call* (London: SIC, 2014), p. 12-13.

[2] Social Integration Commission, *How Integrated is Modern Britain?* 7:12 (London: SIC, 2014),.

[3] These are the latest figures from unpublished research by Brierley Consultancy, scheduled for publication later this year. The most recent published figures from Brierley Consultancy date from 2018 and are higher: nearly 50,000 congregations and over 38,000 in England. Brierley Consultancy, *UK Church Statistics vol. 3: 2018 Edition* 7 (Tonbridge: ADBC Publishers, 2018).

[4] See chapter 1.

[5] While the original data-gathering of this project relates to England alone, secondary data references the UK as a whole where English figures are not available.

[6] T. Cantle, *Community Cohesion: A Report of the Independent Review Team* (London: Home Office, 2001).

[7] Department for Communities and Local Government, *The Government's Response to the Commision on Integration and Cohesion* (Wetherby: Communities and Local Government Publications, 2007), p. 10.

[8] L. Casey, *The Casey Review: A review into opportunity and integration* (London: Department for Communities and Local Government, 2016); R. Bell, N. Plumb, and R. Marangozov, *Integration not demonisation* (London: All Party Parliamentary Ggroup (APPG) on Social Integration, 2017).

[9] See for example, M. Evans, 'British Muslims should not be forced to assimilate, says op counter terror officer', *The Telegraph*, 6 August 2019 www.telegraph.co.uk/politics/2019/08/06/british-muslims-should-not-forced-assimilate-says-senior-counter/; *Find & Connect*, 'Assimilation Policy 1951-62', *Find & Connect* www.findandconnect.gov.au/guide/sa/SE00796

[10] Oxford Consultants for Social Inclusion, *Local Insight: East Lindsey* (Brighton: OSCI, 2019). For a wider discussion of causal links between cohesion and a range of social factors, see also Department for Ministry for Communities and Local Government, *Guidance for local authorities on how to mainstream community cohesion into other services* (Wetherby: Communities and Local Government Publications, 2009).

[11] Onward, *Repairing our social fabric* (London: Onward, 2020), p. 3.

[12] Non-church #320. Throughout this report, participants have been kept anonymous. However, whether they were speaking from with a church setting or otherwise is indicated to help the reader understand the context of their words.

1
From crisis to community: the Church and social cohesion policy

Social cohesion has been near the top of the government's policy agenda for several decades. However, as this chapter will explore, cohesion policy itself has predominantly been developed in response to crisis – and where the distinctive qualities of faith and belief groups have been acknowledged, it has normally been as a risk factor for division. This has had profound implications for how churches (considered as part of the wider faith and belief landscape) are engaged with, and accounted for, by policy-makers and wider society: at best they are neglected, and at worst they are viewed as a problem to be solved. Nonetheless, when we take a longer and wider view – that is, recognising social cohesion as a desirable outcome in its own right, and as something which affects us all whether in crisis or not – a different and more positive view of the church's place in this story starts to emerge.

A crisis-driven approach: faith as a risk factor

British society has changed in various ways over recent decades, both domestically and in its wider engagement with the world. These changes make up the unspoken context through which the cohesion of, and coherence between, local and national communities is navigated:

— The UK is growing more ethnically and culturally diverse. In 1951, just over 4% of the resident UK population was born abroad; by the most recent census in 2011, that figure had risen to 13% (an increase from 1.9 million to 7.5 million people).[13] Patterns of immigration have also changed, and the most recent waves of immigration have particularly seen the share of EEA migrants in employment in the UK increase from around 1.15% in 2004 to around

5.1% in 2017.[14] Notably, immigration has also diversified the faith sector and immigrants are more likely to be religious than the existing UK population; the 2011 census found that 48% of the foreign-born UK population identify as Christian, and 19% as Muslim, while only 14% identified as being non-religious (compared to 25% of the general population in the same poll). More recently, the *British Social Attitudes survey* in 2018-19 found that 52% of the UK population had no religious affiliation; non-religious and minority religious affiliations have increased while Christian affiliation has decreased over recent years.[15]

— At the same time, the existing population has also become increasingly mobile within the UK, particularly as young people move for university or work (with certain areas enjoying an influx of young talent, and others struggling to retain the next generation). Just 26% of people now live within a 15 minute journey of their father and 36% live within 15 minutes of their mother, both having declined by eight percentage points since 2002.[16] In general, we are all becoming less settled – and therefore, less place-bound – than previous generations.

— In 2016, those aged 65 or over made up 15% of the population; by 2041, it is estimated that there will be a further 8.6 million in this age category, making up 26% of the population. The 85+ age group is the fastest growing, and is set to double to 3.2 million in the same period.[17] When coupled with our increasing geographical mobility, the result is often the dislocation of young people and the familial isolation of their ageing relatives.

— These factors contribute to widening economic and cultural differences between regions in the UK. As to the former, recent research from the University of Sheffield has found that only Ireland and Slovakia of the OECD countries are more regionally unequal,[18] and government spending differs by as much as £1,825 per person per year between regions even within England.[19] Regarding the latter, ethnic and cultural diversity is clustered around certain areas of the country, and even within localities: a growing proportion of the minority ethnic population (41% in 2011, up from 25% in 2001) is living in wards where white British citizens are a minority.[20]

— In addition, the UK has one of the highest levels of income inequality in Europe, with the top 20% of households by income receiving 41% of all disposable household income.[21] Particularly in the wake of the COVID-19 pandemic, this inequality is likely to get worse.

Not only have these changes led to diverging experiences between *individuals* over time; when considered alongside natural differences such as those between rural and urban contexts, they also give rise to stark contrasts between *areas* – whether wealthy, poor, diverse, homogenous, 'left behind', or gentrifying – as well as shaping our sense (or otherwise) of shared endeavour in the *nation* as a whole. Meanwhile, the rise of social media and the proliferation of in-home entertainment options – mainly through the influence of the internet – not only further contribute to the loss of shared experience (we no longer all watch the same TV programmes or get our news from the same handful of journalistic outlets) but also reduce our reliance on 'place' for social interaction altogether. On all points, such changes have important implications for social cohesion – and they are long-term shifts in the fabric of our society.

Of course, policymakers have been contending with these shifts as long have they have been occurring. However, it is generally accepted that "community cohesion" as a distinct policy area was established in the wake of a specific moment: the "race riots" which took place across several Northern towns in 2001. The subsequent *Cantle Report* famously observed "parallel lives" between groups in the affected towns, and stressed the need for better opportunities to mix.[22] Some have interpreted these recommendations as the rebuke of an earlier, more *laissez-faire* multiculturalist approach; others view them less dramatically as the "civic-rebalancing" of the same; Cantle himself now advocates for "interculturalism", which distinguishes itself from multiculturalism by greater emphasis on the need to move beyond mere co-existence.[23] For our purposes however, the most important feature of the *Cantle Report* is its emphasis on "bridging" capital between groups (as opposed to "bonding" capital within groups) as the most effective route to a more cohesive society. Moreover, while the *Cantle Report* itself acknowledged the significance of broader socio-economic forces underlying the community separation it observed, the "parallel" groups in question were also of different faiths. Therefore, religion was also subtly implied as a barrier to unimpeded engagement.

> "Community cohesion" as a distinct policy area was established in the wake of the "race riots" which took place across several Northern towns in 2001.

Unfortunately, this has fostered a sense of faith as a problematic source of bonding capital within exclusive identity groups ever since - and the sense of faith as a risk factor and a problem was only compounded by a heightened focus on Islamist radicalisation following 9/11 and the London bombings of July 2005. The line between cohesion policy and a concern for national security has often been blurred as a result.[24] This policy landscape should be viewed in the wider context of the UK's shifting religious demographics, which has led to the gradual racialisation of faith groups in opposition to a perceived secular mainstream. Consequently, issues of 'race and faith' are often viewed together, and with a dominant focus on issues of race, as is reflected for example in the Labour Party's 2017 *Race and Faith Manifesto* which was overwhelmingly focused on issues of racial justice.[25]

Of course, religion can sometimes be divisive and even dangerous; where it is used to support exclusive or violent ideologies it undeniably has a negative impact on social cohesion. However, a disproportionate focus on these legitimate concerns has narrowed our conception of the role of faith and belief groups in society. This legacy is demonstrated by the tone of the landmark *Casey Review* (2016). Three of the five summary points in Casey's "Religion" chapter are concerned with the growth of Islam – including recognition of the "anxiety" caused by the "growth of mosques"– and the prevalence of negative attitudes towards increasing religious diversity in the UK.[26] The most painful consequences of this policy approach have been felt by British Muslims, especially since the introduction of the Prevent Duty in 2015 (which places a legal obligation on certain public authorities to "have a due regard to the need to prevent people from being drawn into terrorism").[27] Yet such a view of religion has also eclipsed a proper consideration of *churches'* distinctive impact on social cohesion (and indeed, of those models of community which maintain space for the co-existence of different values in a shared space). As we shall see, these policy discussions bear little resemblance to churches' engagement with communities on the ground.

More recently, the drawn-out political battle which followed **the 2016 Brexit Referendum** has amounted to a cohesion crisis of a different kind: unlike a riot or terrorist incident, where political attention is focused on minority-majority relations, the last four years have amounted to a process of reckoning for our shared sense of national identity, sorting all of us into two polarised camps and therefore forcing everybody to grapple at some level with cohesion questions. What do we owe each other? Which social and economic communities should be prioritised? And how can we build the common good? The toxicity of this debate led to a rise in reports of hate crime, and even far-right extremism, so significantly broadening the discussion around radicalisation.[28] It has also shone a light on profound disquiet at the perceived imbalances and injustices in the nation's social and political life. Driving the Referendum result, one of our participants (a police leader from Middlesbrough) perceived

> ...a reaction to poverty and the isolation that communities might feel from, you know, Westminster, from the capital, and we're seen as distant, and I think the Brexit vote was, because I watched it and saw it. I saw people queueing up at the polling stations and the strange things were a lot of them were angry. They were coming out to vote and they were angry. And I think, I've never noticed that before in an election.[29]

This sense of regional unfairness particularly reflects some of the more long-term and fundamental societal changes noted above, and positive signs have therefore started to emerge of a more rounded approach to cohesion policy since 2016.[30]

However, as seen from the tone of the *Integrated Communities Action Plan* (published three years after the EU Referendum and still dominated by a suspicion of faith) there is still further to travel: the only mention of faith in the "Places and Communities" section of this Plan is the commitment that "we will develop stronger, more confident communities, running an intensive programme of engagement with communities facing complex issues relating to race and faith".[31] A broader and more nuanced consideration of the churches' contribution is long overdue.

> **A broader and more nuanced consideration of the churches' contribution is long overdue.**

Taking a wider perspective: the churches as a community resource

The political soul-searching prompted by the 2016 Referendum has underlined the obvious truth that behind any flashpoint is a longer story, and a broader approach to cohesion can itself prevent the harmful crisis moments that arise if those stories go unheard. But it also enables us to contextualise cohesion concerns in a more nuanced way.

Yes, there are concerning signs regarding cohesion in the UK. Sadly, as noted in the introduction, the integration of our communities has not kept pace with the changing nature of our society: the 2014 Social Integration Commission compared the recent social interactions of over 4,000 Britons to the social composition of their local areas, and found that on average respondents were 14% less integrated by social grade, 42% less integrated by age, and 48% less integrated by ethnicity than if these factors played no role in their social patterns.[32] By the same measure, London was also found to be less integrated than the rest of Britain. That this should be true of a city so often described as a melting pot, whose diversity is regularly and explicitly lauded as its "strength", reminds us that this social strength is not realised by accident or good intention alone.[33] Rather, cohesion must be nurtured as an end in itself – and through intentional action – if we are to maintain strong social bonds through increasing diversification. A lack of integration can lead to fractured social solidarity, and the think tank Onward has found that 71% of people feel that community has declined in their lifetime.[34]

However, these concerns should be balanced against more positive signs too. For example, while the proportion of people who think people can *generally* be trusted had remained consistently between 40% and 45% in the last four decades, the *British Social Attitudes survey* actually recorded a statistically significant upswing from 47% in 2014 to 54% in 2017 – and the *Community Life Survey 2018-19* also found that 62% of people felt they very strongly or fairly strongly belonged to their local neighbourhood, marking a rise from 58% in 2014–15. Happiness, life satisfaction and "worthwhile" ratings have all increased.[35] Relatedly, when we asked our own participants whether their local areas had moved closer together or further apart in recent years, just over a quarter said further apart, with the remainder judging that their area had moved closer together, stayed the same, or both. Very few mentioned Brexit. The question asked is clearly important – but it would seem that a narrative of declining cohesion dominates our perception of community more than the steady community-building which is happening around us all the time.

Moreover, these positive indications shine through particularly strongly among people of faith – and, it would

seem, especially among frequently practising Christians.
The 2012 Demos report *Faithful Citizens* (drawing in part on
data from the *2010-11 Citizenship Survey*) found that people with
a religious affiliation were more active citizens than those
without: religiously affiliated respondents were more likely
to volunteer regularly, to feel a greater sense of belonging
to their local community and to Britain, and to have higher
levels of trust in people and institutions. This correlation was
strongest among those whose religious identity was important
to them.[36] Furthermore, more recent Theos polling has found
that *frequently practising Christians*
(defined by regular prayer and
church attendance) are the most
likely religious grouping in London
to join a political party, make a
charitable donation, or volunteer
regularly for a local charitable
initiative.[37] Committed Christians
are often quietly attending to what
their communities most need, but
this good work rarely makes the
headlines.

A narrative of declining
cohesion dominates our
perception of community
more than the steady
community-building which
is happening around us all
the time.

**Particularly noteworthy is the Church's response to
austerity,** as more than £30 billion of public spending cuts
over the last decade have seen local churches take on a much
greater role at the frontline of service delivery.[38] Faith-based
volunteer hours rose by almost 60% from 2010-2014, and in 2015
the Cinnamon Network valued this contribution at £3 billion.[39]
Between 2006 and 2016 faith-based charities were the fastest
growing area of the charity sector.[40] Subsequently, research by
Theos and the Church Urban Fund in 2014 found that 10 million
people in the UK had used a church-based community service

that year.[41] The most striking example of the continued strength of Christian involvement since then (and indeed, the sheer extent of the need) is demonstrated by the rise of foodbanks, two thirds of which are now coordinated by the Trussell Trust – a Christian charity founded in 1997, which distributed over 820,000 three-day emergency food parcels in the six months between April and September 2019 alone. This was an increase of 23% on the same period in the previous year – and figures from this year so far suggest usage has vastly increased again in light of the pandemic, with an 89% increase in need for emergency food parcels in April 2020 compared to April 2019.[42] As of 2017, 93% of Anglican churches alone were involved in foodbanks in some way (whether collecting food, providing volunteers or physical space, or giving out vouchers), up from 81% in 2015.[43]

The tensions inherent in church-based service delivery are considered in more detail in chapter three. At this stage, it is sufficient to note how profoundly austerity has affected the role of churches in their communities, as they work to prevent the most vulnerable individuals from falling out of mainstream society – and indeed, therefore, to ensure collective relationships which are characterised by compassion and solidarity. This work has been concerted and growing over recent years. As the founder of a Christian charity in Bolton reflected in November 2018 (long before the current economic crisis) on this remarkable church response:

> We've lost 155 million that's come from the cuts and that's had an impact on a scale unparalleled in history apart from the war. And how does a council, how does a borough, survive? And it survives because there are people who are hungry, and people give their food. And it's not just Christians... but it tends to be Christians or people of faith who create a little bit of a structure to enable that giving to happen... I don't like the recession, but

it is an absolutely fascinating moment in history where we take back our comprehension of community, because it was being professionalised, and our government, our whole institution, took responsibility away from the people, and we are now getting it back. So I think that's why [Christians] have a better space at the table, because I think we're prepared to do it.[44]

That existing government reports have collapsed churches into a problematic caricature of faith as a problem, or a risk factor for division, is therefore especially jarring with the situation on the ground. Moreover, given the depths of hardship that are already emerging as a result of the COVID-19 pandemic, the gap between policy and practice is only likely to increase without conscious reassessment.

From crisis to community: loving your neighbour as a Christian imperative

The figures above identify churches as powerful community resources marked by compassion for, and solidarity with, their local neighbourhoods – and indeed, at a practical level, many of our participants stressed that they had made the most powerful impact on their local areas precisely where they had made special effort to listen before acting (that is, tailoring their community engagement to the neighbourhoods in which they were serving).[45] Again, this is the very opposite of a crisis-based approach, requiring deep listening, dialogue, and iteration. It can be fostered through informal conversation, pre-existing local knowledge,

> Given the depths of hardship that are already emerging as a result of the COVID-19 pandemic, the gap between policy and practice is only likely to increase without conscious reassessment.

or even formal consultation of local needs, as one parish priest in Bradford (a council-based monitoring and evaluation officer by professional background) undertook, as a way of gathering evidence for fundraising to build a new community hall. In demonstrating that there was local support for his church's building plans, he was able to raise over £160,000 over three years to build the hall, which is now a community hub in one of the most deprived parishes in the country.[46] Across our sample, and in a range of sectors, churches themselves were praised where tailoring was prioritised, and criticised if it was felt they had rushed into projects without proper consideration of the wider community landscape.[47]

> **Many of our church-based participants' responses were imbued with a profoundly theological sense of how neighbour-love might be reflected in practical engagement with literal neighbours.**

Churches are extremely well-placed to listen and iterate their community presence, but where does their motivation for community engagement come from in the first place? To this end, it is pertinent to note the observation of the *Cantle Report* itself, that

> *It is unfashionable to speak of loving one's neighbour, but unless our society can move at least to a position where we can respect our neighbours as fellow human beings, we shall fail in our attempts to create a harmonious society in which conditions have changed so radically in the last 40 years.*[48]

Demonstrably, it must be said, churches have not given up on this "unfashionable" ideal. On the contrary, to "love your neighbour as yourself" remains a central Christian

imperative,[49] and our researchers were struck by how many of
our church-based participants' responses were imbued with
a profoundly theological sense of how this neighbour-love
might be reflected in practical engagement with literal
neighbours. Common themes were the need to follow Christ's
example,[50] the call to be "salt and light" in the community,[51]
bringing the marginalised into the centre,[52] building the
Kingdom,[53] and love of neighbour.[54] In short, churches have
their own authentically Christian reasons to care deeply about
social cohesion. A sample of these theological reflections is
offered in the box below.

**Theological reflections: social cohesion in the churches'
own words**

[Social cohesion is] kind of the leaking out of loving your
neighbour... I think you will find that individuals will visit
people who are sick, will stay in touch with people who are
housebound, will set up little coffee mornings, and you know. It
just is the lifeblood of the church. It's what it does. Because it's
about loving your neighbour, really.[55] (Anglican Priest, Derby.)

And you could take it up to Jeremiah's instruction in Jeremiah
29, where he said, "We should get involved, we should build
houses, we should build schools..." That's my paraphrase.
"And we should get involved in the economic well-being of
the city, because if it prospers, we prosper".... And I think it
goes on to answer the big question of who is your neighbour?
The Good Samaritan. And I think that when we understand
those theologies, it will help us to kind of appreciate the fact
that it's not Church, per se. It's Kingdom more than Church,
and Kingdom is bigger than Church.[56] (Independent Pastor,
Croydon.)

I think [social cohesion work] is right at the top [in a list of the Church's priorities]. I think it's entirely about relationships and friendship... I think social justice is a strange term in the sense that, if we mean that we have a foodbank, well that's great – but do we have relationships in that? Are we doing that in the context of relationships or just handing stuff out? I think social cohesion is much more important because also the whole community is much better equipped to look after an individual than one or two of us.[57] (Anglican Priest, Plymouth.)

[Social cohesion] is a theological task... and it should be about how we live faith. We are aiming to be all children of God, neither Jew nor Greek, slave nor free, all are together. And so that's a deeply theological purpose for the church.[58] (Anglican Cathedral-based Priest, Peterborough.)

I didn't really see the significance of food, but it seems to be so important whenever you bring people together. It's like the Lord's Supper, with the breaking of bread and the wine. There's something that's supernatural about it, and that – you know, Jesus brings people together. He's magnetic. Whenever Jesus appeared in the Bible, crowds would go to him! And there's something about that, you know? So I feel it is important to bring people together.[59] (Non-denominational local church leader, Bolton.)

It seems so fundamental that [Jesus] wanted to be so inclusive, and often those who are most marginalized – either women, or Samaritans, or you know, the people we don't normally mix with, or people who are excluded for some reason.... You know, he actively went out and invited people and sought them. And I think that people have an image of church that you have to be – it can become bit like a social club – you have to be a certain way to fit in and tick all the boxes. And actually it should be the opposite of that, really.[60] (Anglican lay volunteer, Haringey.)

Jesus said "Your kingdom come, Your will be done on earth as it is in heaven", and so bringing his Kingdom is to me about seeing lives transformed, seeing cities transformed which is obviously an extension of that, seeing communities come together, seeing places become more peaceful, crime drop. You know, kinds of stuff that looks like heaven invading earth essentially. Or, you know, "The Kingdom come on earth as it is in heaven".[61] (Christian radio DJ, Plymouth.)

So with cohesion, I think of gluing together, being a kind of a glue... The word religion at root means to bind together — religare. That's a lovely idea of what religion is at root: to bind people together. People who are from here, there and everywhere, we're all kind of human beings together.[62] (Prison chaplaincy professional.)

I think that's what it means to be Catholic. You could say that that's exactly what katholos (Catholic) means: that different people come together with the same faith – the same relationship – that unites them all. And we do people a disservice by allowing them to exist in their units, you know.[63] (Catholic Church Leader, Newham.)

While deeply embedded in and committed to their communities then, churches should not be considered simply as generic community groups. Rather, they are a distinctive part of the social fabric whose religious motivation inescapably characterises the scale and scope of their practical contribution. As one Senior Policy Advisor for a council reflected:

It's been a learning relationship with the faith sector over the last 18 months, sometimes out of necessity a little bit. But I'm always a bit in awe of how in touch they are with human beings compared to my organisation which sometimes loses that... I think there's a real sense of love for the people they work after, but also the place they look after. And that emotional attachment to anywhere is never a [negative] thing.[64]

That this non-church-based participant associates a "sense of love for... people" with an 'emotional attachment to place' is a pertinent observation of faith-motivated neighbour-love. To this end, while Christians do not only define their neighbour in literal terms (often speaking of our obligations to our "global neighbours" too) it is perhaps most obviously expressed in the 'parochial' model. This is the system operated by a number of denominations (and from which various others derive their own local-national organisational models) whereby the entirety of the country is divided into 'parishes', each of which is overseen by a priest with responsibility for the spiritual life of the whole community – not just the congregation. At the same time, such deeply grounded sense of care for one's community is an outlook, not a particular organisational structure – and, as we shall see, our research found this same parochial (as opposed to 'congregational') attitude in many churches without a formal parish structure.

Conclusion

Cohesion policy has generally been driven forward in response to crisis, and a generic understanding of faith as a risk factor for division has prevented a nuanced consideration of churches' distinctive contribution. Nonetheless, a different picture emerges when we move away from this crisis-based approach: a picture of quiet yet consistent cohesion work happening all the time, with churches at the forefront of the community response.

We have noted that being receptive to the community and tailoring one's cohesion response accordingly is critical when looking beyond the next crisis – and churches are well-equipped to prioritise this active listening, given that they spring forth from their local neighbourhoods, rather than acting in separation from them. But going further, if churches are not just generic community groups (as this chapter has argued) what are the particular ingredients of their social cohesion contribution, and are they being utilised to their full potential? Put another way, what are the assets that churches actually offer their communities in pursuit of a more cohesive society?

Being receptive to the community and tailoring one's cohesion response accordingly is critical when looking beyond the next crisis – and churches are well-equipped to prioritise this active listening.

It is with this question in mind that chapter two will consider churches' contributions in more granular detail, identifying their major assets and assessing how effectively (or otherwise) they are being mobilised across England to nurture social cohesion. In doing so, the discussion is informed by the approach of asset-based community development (ABCD), which seeks to identify and build on existing assets in order to realise potential within the community, and which has become increasingly popular in the voluntary sector. ABCD is often contrasted with a needs-based approach (that is, an approach which sees problems and then works to solve them).[65] However, the Commission does not seek to prioritise one over the other: as above, it is recognised that tailoring one's response to real need is demonstrably a good thing, and it is a strength of churches that they are well-placed to do this well as institutions embedded in their own communities. Instead, the report draws insight from both needs- and asset-based approaches to benefit from the wisdom of each. Having recognised the importance of churches' embeddedness in community and the quiet cohesion work it nurtures, therefore, it is to a more detailed consideration of the churches' cohesion contribution through a consideration of its assets that we now turn.

[13] C. Smith, '2011 Census analysis: Immigration Patterns of Non-UK Born Populations in England and Wales in 2011', *Office for National Statistics*, 17 December 2013. www.ons.gov.uk/peoplepopulationandcommunity/ populationandmigration/internationalmigration/articles/ immigrationpatternsofnonukbornpopulationsinenglandandwalesin2011 /2013-12-17

[14] Migration Advisory Committee, *EEA migration in the UK: Final report* (London: MAC, 2018), p. 10.

[15] J. Curtice, E. Clery, J. Perry, M. Phillips and N. Rahim (eds.), *British Social Attitudes: the 36th Report* (London: NatCen Social Research, 2019), p. 5; R. O'Brien and A. Potter-Collins, '2011 Census Analysis: Ethnicity and Religion of the Non-UK Born Population in England and Wales', *Office for National Statistics*, 18 June 2015. www.ons.gov.uk/peoplepopulationandcommunity/culturalidentity/ethnicity/ les/2011censusanalysisethnicityandreligionofthenonukbornpopulationinen glandandwales/2015-06-18

[16] Onward, *Repairing our Social Fabric*, p. 16.

[17] *Age UK*, 'Later Life in the United Kingdom, 2019', *Age UK*, May 2019. www.ageuk.org.uk/globalassets/age-uk/documents/ reports-and-publications/later_life_uk_factsheet.pdf

[18] P. McCann, 'Perceptions of regional inequality and the geography of discontent: insights from the UK', *Regional Studies*, 54:2 (2019), pp. 256- 267. www.tandfonline.com/doi/full/10.1080/00343404.2019.1619928

[19] The discrepancy is even higher between the four nations of the UK, though the scope of the public sector differs between nations (for example, the water supply is within the public sector in Northern Ireland and Scotland, but the private sector in England and Wales). P. Brien, 'Public spending by country and region', *House of Commons Library*, 13 December 2019. commonslibrary.parliament.uk/research-briefings/sn04033/

[20] E. Kaufmann, *Half Full or Half Empty?: How Has Ethnic Segregation in England and Wales Changed Between 2001 and 2011* (London: Demos, 2013), p. 2. www.demos.co.uk/files/ethnicdistributione+w.pdf

[21] F. McGuinness and D. Harari, 'Income Inequality in the UK' (London: House of Commons, 2019), p. 14, 23-24. commonslibrary.parliament.uk/ researchbriefings/cbp-7484; P. Bourquin et al., *Living standards, poverty and inequality in the UK: 2019* (London: Institute for Fiscal Studies, 2019), p. 16-18.

[22] Cantle, *Community Cohesion*, p. 9.

[23] A. Kundnani, 'The Death of Multiculturalism', *Race and Class*, 43:4 (2002), pp. 67-72; N. Meer and T. Modood, 'The Multicultural State We're In: Muslims, "Multiculture" and the "Civic-Rebalancing" of British Multiculturalism', *Political Studies*, 57:3 (2009), pp. 473-497; T. Cantle, *Interculturalism: The New Era of Cohesion*

and Diversity (Basingstoke: Palgrave, 2013); M. Antonsich, 'Interculturalism versus multiculturalism – the Cantle-Modood debate' *Ethnicities*, 16:3 (2016), pp. 470-493.

[24] For a more extensive discussion of these policy discussions, see M. Pennington, *Cohesive Societies: Faith and Belief* (London: British Academy and the Faith and Belief Forum, 2020), p. 15-22.

[25] The Labour Party, *Race and Faith Manifesto* (The Labour Party, 2017).

[26] Casey, *The Casey Review*, p. 121.

[27] HM Government, *Prevent duty guidance*, (London: HM Government, 2015). www. legislation.gov.uk/ukdsi/2015/9780111133309/pdfs/ukdsiod_9780111133309_

en.pdf

[28] Reported hate crimes have risen steadily in recent years, with notable peaks around key events including the 2016 EU Referendum. However, these figures should be interpreted cautiously: the Crime Survey (a randomly-selected and representative set of 50,000 households) suggest numbers of people identifying themselves as victims of hate crimes *decreased* over the same period. Far-right extremism is nonetheless acknowledged as a growing threat by the Home Office and, as of 2019, five of the top 10 far-right activists with the biggest global reach were British citizens. Home Office, *Hate Crime, England and Wales 2017/18* (London: *Office of National Statistics*, 16 October 2018), assets.publishing. service.gov.uk/government/uploads/system/uploads/attachment_data/ file/748598/hate-crime-1718-hosb2018.pdf; HOPE not Hate, *State of Hate 2019: People vs. the Elite?* (London: HOPE not Hate, 2019)p. 3. www.hopenothate. org.uk/wp-content/uploads/2019/02/state-of-hate-2019-final-1.pdf

[29] Non-church #39.

[30] Above all, in the work of the APPG on Social Integration, founded in 2016. See, for example, APPG on Social Integration, *Ages Apart? Ties and Divides Across the Generations* (2017), APPG on Social Integration, *Healing the Generational Divide: Interim report on intergenerational connection* (2019).

[31] Ministry for Housing, Communities and Local Government, *Integrated Communities Action Plan* (London: Crown, 2019), p. 14-15, 18-19.

[32] These figures were reached by comparing the recent social interactions of over 4,200 Britons to what we might expect those interactions to look like based on the social composition of their local neighbourhoods. For example if 30% of a white respondent's social interactions were with people who were not white, but they lived in an area where 40% of the residents were not white, they would be 25% less integrated by ethnicity than if ethnicity had been irrelevant to their social patterns. Social Integration Commission, *How Integrated is Modern Britain?* p. 7, 12.

[33] Ibid. 7; S. Khan, *Twitter*, 18 June 2019 twitter.com/ SadiqKhan/status/1141087248529707008

[34] Onward, *Repairing Our Social Fabric*, p. 7.

[35] D. Phillips, J. Curtice, M. Phillips, and J. Perry (eds.) 'Social trust', *British Social Attitudes 35* (London: The National Centre for Social Research, 2018) www.bsa.natcen.ac.uk/media/39278/bsa35_social_trust.pdf; Department for Digital, Culture, Media and Sport, *Community Life Survey 2018-19* (London: Department for Digital, Culture, Media and Sport, 2019), p. 14. assets.publishing.service.gov.uk/government/uploads/system/uploads/attachment_data/file/820610/Community_Life_Survey_2018-19_report.pdf; Onward, *Repairing Our Social Fabric*, p. 6-7.

[36] J. Birdwell, *Faithful Citizens* (London: Demos, 2012), p. 16-21. demosuk.wpengine.com/files/Faithful_citizens_-_web.pdf?1333839181; Communities and Local Government, *Citizenship Survey: April 2010-March 2011, England –* Tables (London: Communities and Local Government, 2011), tables 9 and 11. webarchive.nationalarchives.gov.uk/20120919165040/http://www.communities.gov.uk/publications/corporate/statistics/citizenshipsurveyq4201011

[37] P. Bickley and N. Mladin, *Religious London* (London: Theos, 2020), p. 55. www.theosthinktank.co.uk/cmsfiles/Religious-London-FINAL-REPORT-24.06.2020.pdf

[38] or a summary of the impact of austerity on local government spending in the UK, see Joseph Rowntree Foundation, *The cost of the cuts: the impact on local government and poorer communities* (York: JRF, 2015). www.jrf.org.uk/sites/default/files/jrf/migrated/files/Summary-Final.pdf; B. Mueller, 'What is Austerity And How Has It Affected British Society?', *New York Times*, 24 February 2019. www.nytimes.com/2019/02/24/world/europe/britain-austerity-may-budget.html

[39] The *2016 Cinnamon Faith Audit* assessed the impact of faith groups across the country, as well as leading to a series of supplementary audits at a local authority level. G. Knott, *Investing More for the Common Good: National Church Social Action Survey Results 2014* (Shrewsbury: Jubilee Plus, 2014), p. 2; Cinnamon Network, *Cinnamon Faith Action Audit* (London: Cinnamon Faith Action Research, 2016), p. 2.

[40] R. Wright, 'How churches are filling the gap left by austerity cuts', *Financial Times*, 19 April 2019. www.ft.com/content/f5890a4e-6140-11e9-b285-3acd5d43599e; Nick Spencer, *Doing Good* (London: Theos, 2016), p. 44-45.

[41] P. Bickley, *Good Neighbours: How Churches Help Communities Flourish* (London: Church Urban Fund, 2015), p. 10.

[42] Trussell Trust, 'Steepest increase in people needing food banks for past 5 years as need soars by 23%', 13 November 2019. www.trusselltrust.org/2019/11/13/april-sept-2019-foodbank-figures/; Trussell Trust, 'Summary Findings on the Impact of the Covid-19 Crisis on Food Banks', June 2020. www.trusselltrust.org/wp-content/uploads/sites/2/2020/06/APRIL-Data-briefing_external.pdf

[43] Church Urban Fund, *Church in Action: A National Survey* (London: Church Urban Fund, 2017), p. 8. cuf.org.uk/uploads/resources/Church_in_Action_Exec_Summary_Cover_2017.pdf; Church Urban Fund, *Church in Action: A National Survey of Church-Based Social Action* (London: Church Urban Fund, 2015), 12-13. cuf.org.uk/uploads/resources/Church-in-Action-2015_0.pdf

[44] Church #13.

[45] E.g. Non-church #145, Non-church #195, Non-church #271, Non-church #275, Church #52, Church #74, Church #176, Church #355, Church #300.

[46] Church #245.

[47] Church #304.

[48] Cantle, *The Cantle Report*, p. 20.

[49] Matthew 22:37-39.

[50] Church #173, Church #52, Church #245.

[51] Church #126, Church #42, Church #180, Church #18, Church #280.

[52] Church #109, Church #277, Church #353.

[53] Church #180, Church #166, Church #38, Church #88, Church #108, Church #171.

[54] Church #190, Church #170, Church #322, Church #11, Church #171.

[55] Church #222.

[56] Church #126.

[57] Church #88.

[58] Church #193.

[59] Church #3.

[60] Church #109.

[61] Church #180.

[62] Church #353.

[63] Church #88.

[64] Church #174.

[65] For example, A. Mathie and G. Cunningham, 'Who is Driving Development? Reflections on the Transformative Potential of Asset-based Community Development', *Canadian Journal of Development Studies*, 26:1 (2005), pp. 175-186; A. Mathie and G. Cunningham, 'From clients to citizens: Asset-based Community Development as a strategy for community-driven development', *Development in Practice*, 13:5 (2003, pp. 474-486.

2

Church assets

A consideration of churches' assets does not deny the depth of need in many of our communities, but it is a helpful counterpoint to crisis-driven cohesion policy because it encourages long-term and sustainable action, enabling a response that is authentically rooted in churches' own character even as it meets the concerns of wider society. This sort of creative reflection on the natural assets in a community has been particularly welcome in a time of reduced public spending,[66] and to this end, it is perhaps telling that among our church-based participants, explicit language of "assets" was used predominantly by those with some form of regional strategic responsibility (i.e. those who were more commonly in conversation with other sectors). From regional Anglican leaders in Middlesbrough and Plymouth respectively, for example, we heard:

> ...one of the things that we have to be really mindful of when we're thinking about the Church's involvement in things is capacity and resources... what's developed and has emerged has been because – I suppose it's this asset-based approach, really. There's somebody like [Anon.] saying, "I've got a huge asset, a huge resource here, and it's not doing what it could do. How can we use it?" Now, that's a very obvious thing because it was a building. Sometimes it's people who just have a vision or a passion for something. [67]

> We work very much from an asset-based approach, and people say to me but what does that mean? It's like well, can you talk to people? Yeah. Can you make a cup of tea? Asset-based development, you know. You're using what you have, to share. [68]

Nonetheless, across all interviews – both church-based and otherwise – we found several key features of the church's response emerging again and again, reflecting the most common resources that pro-active churches drew upon to improve the cohesiveness of their communities. We can group these features into six themes: (1) buildings, (2) networks, (3) leadership, (4) volunteers, (5) convening power, and (6) vision. This chapter will consider each in turn, uncovering the ways in which churches are directing their assets towards good cohesion outcomes – as well as ways in which they can be used less positively, to hold back or even undermine cohesive societies.

Buildings: churches as places of gathering

At the time of writing, group physical gathering is significantly restricted by the ongoing COVID-19 pandemic. Yet even before the onset of this current crisis, communities across the country were already struggling with a notable and rapid decline of community space; whether the country gets 'back to normal' sooner or later, many of our public buildings have already been lost over recent years.[69]

More than 600 youth centres and clubs closed across Britain over the last six years, leading to the loss of 3,650 dedicated staff and 139,000 places on youth programmes; council-run community centres have also dramatically reduced in number.[70]

So too, between 2001 and 2018, the number of pubs fell by 26% (the UK now has more church buildings than pubs) and since 2005 the number of public libraries fell by 27%.[71] Reflecting on this decline, one council officer in Croydon noted that:

> There is an issue with council – well not just council, but building, assets. And I think people assume that the council has

loads of buildings that anyone can use, and can just rent them for cheap or for free, and that isn't the case... If you're a community organisation or a church or something that might want space to use to do something for your community, that is quite hard to find those spaces I think.[72]

In this context, many churches are extremely well-positioned to provide gathering points – often hosting the only shared space in an area, particularly in rural or deprived contexts. Moreover, since they are scattered across communities, they serve isolated villages and suburbs as directly as town centres and city metropoles.[73] As of 2018, there were an estimated 42,000 dedicated church buildings across the UK, in addition to many church-owned community spaces not used specifically for worship.[74] These buildings are not spread evenly across different Christian traditions, and not all churches have their own premises. However, when taken as a whole, the community impact of church buildings is highly positive.

66

Even before the onset of this current crisis, communities across the country were already struggling with a notable and rapid decline of community space.

Above all, they host a vast range of community activities. From a cohesion perspective, these can be categorised broadly in three groups:

— Facilitating social connection: simple socialising for its own sake, which may encourage bonding capital (e.g. youth groups, elderly social clubs, parent and toddler sessions, LGBT+ drop ins) or bridging capital (e.g. community cafés and coffee mornings);

— **Tackling material need:** meeting a specific and immediate material need which might have a knock-on impact on local cohesion (e.g. foodbanks, homeless shelters, English language classes, pre-schools, asylum seeker and refugee drop-ins, addiction support, debt advice, community midwife provision, and counselling);

— **Promoting common endeavour:** otherwise diverse groups gathering because of a pre-existing shared concern or common interest (e.g. art, philosophy and bridge clubs, dance classes, choirs and even a permanent art collective).

None of these activities would happen without a place to gather, and each brings its own cohesion benefit – whether through combatting isolation and loneliness, ensuring the integration into wider society of those on the margins, or simply bringing people of diverse backgrounds together around something practical. Such gatherings are meaningful from a cohesion perspective whether or not they are responding to urgent material need, and in all cases – including those activities which focus on the bonding of an in-group, but nevertheless draw people together along other differences – direct personal interaction is encouraged outside one's immediate social circle. This is strongly associated with good cohesion outcomes on the basis of 'Contact Theory', whereby hostility between different groups is reduced through positive interpersonal contact.[75] Of one family drop-in service in Middlesbrough, attended by families of various different ethnicities and religions, the church-employed facilitator said:

> *When you get to know [people], and you get to know their name, and something about their character, them and us disappears. And that's my hope for [this group]: that you stop seeing the colour of their skin, or you stop seeing the fact that*

they cover the hair up, or that they have a bindi here, and you just see a person. We're all people.[76]

The attendees in this example were similar according to one characteristic (i.e. they were young families) and far from being a cohesion problem, this was the very reason they gathered at all. However, at the same time, they were also diverse in a number of other ways, and the drop-in was therefore meaningfully able to promote bridging opportunities in the local area. That bonding capital according to one criterion can facilitate bridging capital according to others is vital to understanding the full extent of the churches' impact on social cohesion.

Looking forward to a time when buildings are able to reopen without public health restrictions, it is worth noting that very few of our participants seemed to have tried *proactively* to bring together different external groups using the building at the same time: most community groups just use buildings for their own purposes and leave. By taking a more pro-active approach, churches could maximise the cohesion benefits of existing good work even further with relatively little additional effort on their own part. However, in the meantime the pandemic has clearly necessitated that most of this contact must happen in other ways (or not at all). It is worth noting that many church premises have still hosted community response hubs, for example foodbanks, through lockdown. A church survey conducted by the National Churches Trust suggests that 89% of churches continued to provide some form of community support throughout, and the top new activity was making contact with isolated or vulnerable people.[77] Nonetheless, churches' capacity to encourage serendipitous or casual in-person meeting in their buildings is almost entirely restricted by current regulations: the same report showed that only 34% had continued their support in full, and respondents said they were most looking forward to "companionship/togetherness" when churches reopened, reiterating the gap in merely social gathering caused by the pandemic.[78] The cohesion impact of physical meeting versus online meeting is yet to be established.

Throughout our research, community-based participants especially praised churches for offering their space cheaply or for free. Since church buildings are present in every community (rather than being centralised like many statutory services), this supplements schemes which run only in built up centres and require travel to attend – a particular barrier to engagement for those with the most limited resources (for example those who cannot afford a bus fare, or with particular accessibility requirements).

> That bonding capital according to one criterion can facilitate bridging capital according to others is vital to understanding the full extent of the churches' impact on social cohesion.

To some extent, it also mitigates the effects of the regional funding disparities noted in chapter one and enables groups which are publicly funded to spend their money on enhancing their activities rather than underwriting their basic viability. With this in mind, we came across several churches running different payment policies for different groups; charging structures might depend, for example, on whether they were making a profit or not, or whether they had only recently started (as a way of helping new groups to grow).[79]

A small number of church-based participants did criticise their own local churches for charging too highly for space. For example, one participant in Solihull reflected that:

> *[The church is] hired out a lot for use in the community, but it's hired out for profit... it is used as a means of support. [The church] couldn't manage if it didn't get that income... If for some reason we couldn't hire it out, then people would dig into their own pockets, I'm sure, to keep it going, but they don't at the moment. It's "Oh well, we use the building to make money out of it."* [80]

If churches can afford to lower their prices for initiatives which benefit the community, they should consider doing so. However, this is not always a simple choice. As this participant acknowledged, church buildings are not free to maintain and the responsibility for their maintenance usually lies with the local congregation. This extract from an interview with a Salvation Army leader in Croydon illustrates the scale of the challenge facing local congregations:

> *We're coming to the end of the working life of this building and we need to build a new building. We need new facilities, and that's probably somewhere in the region of about £4.5 million. The church has got about £20,000, so there's quite a deficit.* [81]

Rental income can be an important financial supplement, and it is worth noting the recent experience of the Saint John Paul II Pastoral Centre in Middlesbrough here. The Centre provided a site for various charitable activities in support of vulnerable groups in the town, including refugees and homeless people, and was praised by many of our participants for its work. However, it was forced to close in February 2020 after adjustments required to bring its electrical and fire safety provision in line with latest requirements were deemed unaffordable.[82]

Therefore, buildings can become "white elephants" for congregations – so much so that we came across several instances where the destruction of local churches by fire had been experienced as a process of release and renewal by the congregation, who felt liberated to consider their mission without such a pressing burden.[83]   Certainly, preoccupation with maintenance can come at the expense of human flourishing in other ways:

> I wrote to my people [asking for the release of funds to pay for the funeral of the churchwarden who died suddenly without family] and all but one said "No. Not the church's responsibility. The money we have is for the buildings." I almost quit. I just thought, what am I doing here? We are not the National Trust.[84]

> It becomes all about the building: "Church is the building, and we want it to look pristine. It doesn't matter if people go there or not. It is about the building." So, there is not really a concept of mission and outreach.[85]

Neither are church buildings always conducive to wider community use. The inflexibility of pews and the difficulties of making adjustments to old buildings (which are often listed) can limit what a church is able to offer.[86] Some participants also expressed concern around the perceived neutrality of church space – for example, one young Christian widely involved in local community work reflected that she would not hold a "spoken word" poetry youth event at her church "because people often feel strange going into a church".[87] Nonetheless, these concerns were usually reported second-hand (i.e. "I worry other people perceive X") rather than personal. Conversely, the inclusive and welcoming ethos of church buildings was often mentioned, to the extent that one non-Christian council officer with oversight of children and family services observed:

> Where do people get their hope? Where do people get their support from? Where do people get compassion from? Well you'll find all of those things in a church, whether you believe or not. You don't always find that in a public sector building, because they are about telling you why you don't meet the threshold, why you can't access the services, and why you need to pull yourself up by the bootstraps and get on with it.[88]

The recognisably Christian nature of church buildings can also generate its own unexpected opportunities to foster cohesion between people of different backgrounds. One participant described how many visitors to their church building had "been in other countries where a church has helped them and they'll see the spire and they will come", so that:

> On a Monday we might have 30 older Pakistani ladies in, and 15 Iranian men, and five Congolese Africans. They're all in [the building] together and I think they just realise they're not actually all that different, so we have African ladies that are Christian but wear hijabs... and then we have Pakistani ladies who might choose not to wear a headscarf, and then Iranian ladies that were Muslim but are now Christian. So it's a whole mix of different people and they ask questions of each other.[89]

This church was situated in an area of Bradford that had experienced riots in 1995 – so the Christian visibility of the building offered an opportunity to bring together different residents in an area with historically strained community relations. That churches might have such inroads into immigrant and emerging communities will only become more significant to the nation's cohesion strategy as the demographics of faith change, given higher levels of religiosity among the immigrant population (as noted above).[90]

This should also serve as a reminder of the cohesion challenges facing those congregations without their own designated worship space – many of which, though by no means all, are immigrant churches. For example, one Free Church leader told us they had tried to conduct a baptism in the local swimming pool as they had no other option, but were banned from doing so.[91] After all, church buildings are not distributed equally across the range of Christian traditions, and the stereotypical image of a quaint Anglican parish church reflects an increasingly narrow segment of English Christianity: the largest proportion of Christian buildings are Anglican, but many thriving congregations rent third-party space in which to worship, and these same groups often represent the main growth areas in English Christianity (especially in London) by faith affiliation.[92] Without a designated building, churches can obviously still engage with their communities, but they can usually only do so while being hosted in others' space, or through supporting third-party projects. Meanwhile, those churches with their own buildings are able to take on the role of host.

So too, buildings can be assumed by those outside the church to indicate greater legitimacy, and those churches without a visible, public space of their own can therefore be the focus of greater suspicion from others (especially relating to concerns around safeguarding compliance) while nonetheless taking their legal responsibilities seriously and generating vital feelings of belonging among their congregations – particularly for those recently arrived in the UK.[93] Of course, some concerns around safeguarding within churches are entirely justified, but this does not correlate to whether churches have their own buildings or not.

Churches looking for third-party space need to be able to demonstrate that they take safeguarding seriously, and that they are accountable beyond their own leadership; meanwhile, organisations which do own buildings, including other churches, should consider how their use of these buildings could be used to support such groups to worship freely and visibly as part of an accepting and cohesive society.[94] This is a particular concern in urban areas (i.e. those areas with the most diverse faith sectors) though new church communities are emerging in rural areas as well, and this trend is likely to increase as the shape of Christianity in this country continues to change.[95]

All that said, it would be a woeful misrepresentation to assume that church-based activities merely represent savvy rental opportunities for churches. As a recent Theos report noted, church buildings are an important source of physical capital, but their full "significance for resilience only emerges by understanding [the] dynamic combination of the spaces themselves and the things that happen in them – the way that they are 'enacted'."[96] To this end, a large proportion of initiatives which occur in church space are delivered in-house, fuelled by a deep spiritual commitment to the wider community, and in a coordinated way, with churches consciously running projects in these spaces that try to meet the holistic needs of their neighbours. Congregations will often invest significant time and money (and time to raise money!) in enhancing their space for community usage. This could be installing or upgrading basic kitchen facilities,[97] but in some cases, it is more targeted towards a specific activity in mind. We encountered two instances where churches had converted whole sections of their buildings into soft play areas for local children – and in both instances, the churches have continued providing online resources for children's activities during the COVID-19 lockdown, demonstrating their enduring concern to serve the youngest members of their communities, even without physical assets.[98]

In turn, church buildings are often loved by their communities. One community worker in Bolton reflected on the recent history of the Anglican church at St Chad's, Tonge Fold, which was marked for closure by its diocese in 2015, and had not had a permanent vicar since October 2017, but was saved following a campaign in the wider community to keep it open:

> A large proportion of initiatives which occur in church space are delivered in-house, fuelled by a deep spiritual commitment to the wider community, and in a coordinated way, with churches consciously running projects in these spaces that try to meet the holistic needs of their neighbours.

> *What's just gorgeous about the story of this church is that actually the community who weren't church members – who aren't religious, who had no intention of going to church, who are from different religions – were like "Do you know what? I don't want the church to close down. It's a great building, I really want to support the church."* [99]

The church runs a diverse programme of community events in one of the most deprived parishes in the country (Tonge Fold ranks 1174th out of 12382, where 1 is most deprived), and its small congregation sustains this programme through the input of a committed group of volunteers from beyond the church – including several volunteers active in other non-Christian faith communities. The church has become a focal point for this neighbourhood's shared life.

In this way, church buildings can become a vehicle for cultural memory and a sense of shared local identity – both of which help foster positive feelings of belonging in the community. On this point, cathedrals are especially well-placed to hold the story, identity and memory of communities – as was illustrated to devastating effect by the (international) outpouring of grief following the 2019 Notre Dame fire, which occurred during this research. The symbolic significance of cathedrals was noted by various non-church participants in this study,[100] reiterating the findings of the 2012 Theos report *Spiritual Capital*, which noted the particular capacity of cathedrals to connect with those beyond the confines of Christianity, promote bridging capital as community hubs, and embody local identity and history for the whole community. Polling from that report found that 59% of the public agreed that "[Anglican] Cathedrals belong to the whole, not just the Church of England" and 56% felt they were "important symbols of identity in their community".[101] Cathedrals are also a popular site for interfaith engagement, and one Muslim leader in Bradford told us they had been involved in the organisation of a series of events at the Cathedral specifically "to show [non-Christians] that it's a building that's not just for the Christian community".[102]

Networks: churches as the "capillaries" of community

The emotional and symbolic reach of church buildings points to the fact that churches are not only embedded physically, but socially, in their communities. As such, one church leader strikingly described churches as the "capillary" level of the community. Capillaries form the circulatory network which delivers nourishment at a scale unreachable by other means, making life possible.[103]

In the first instance, diverse and far-reaching church-based networks form through worship itself, and Christian congregations can be extremely varied by age, socio-economic group, ethnicity, and even nationality. Once again, bonding capital in one sense (i.e. faith) can facilitate bridging capital according to others (e.g. age, ethnicity or socio-economic background) in the setting of worship; one church we visited in Derby told us 50 nationalities were represented in their congregation and a church in Newham was reported to welcome congregants from 187 countries, though these are rare extremes and the extent of diversity of course differs greatly between different churches and church traditions.[104]

One church leader strikingly described churches as the "capillary" level of the community.

Greater homogeneity is unavoidable where churches are based in non-diverse areas, but can also arise where they are associated with a particular national group or even tribe: one pastor told us of a Nigerian family who travelled far to join his congregation rather than attending the large Nigerian church close to their house, because it was associated with a different tribal group than their own.[105] We also heard concerns specifically from several Catholic participants about the impact of nation-based Catholic congregations (for example, a Polish Catholic Church and an English Catholic Church) developing alongside one another rather than together, especially when the global and diverse nature of Catholic congregations was otherwise recognised as a particular strength (though it is significant to note that other participants, including those outside Catholicism, viewed this as a sign of welcoming and positive provision for minority communities, and separate congregations often had positive working relationships).[106]

It is also important to note that over the course of the Commission, concerns over the perceived failure of the Church of England to reckon with institutional racism have particularly made national news. Issues at stake have been a lack of solidarity around matters of racial justice, a specific failure to welcome members of the Windrush generation, and an ongoing lack of representation and diversity among both congregations and clergy. At a General Synod meeting in February 2020, a motion apologising for "the conscious and unconscious racism experienced by countless black, Asian and minority ethnic (BAME) Anglicans in 1948 and subsequent years" was unanimously backed, and committed to a formal, independent review of the issue.[107]

So, healthy relationships between bonding and bridging are often thriving in church settings, and the extent of this phenomenon is underappreciated. However, where this balance is not appreciated and nurtured by the congregations themselves, like any groups, churches can become more inward-looking or exclusive.

More positively, outside worship, church-based networks are bolstered and extended through church-run events. The *2016 Cinnamon Faith Audit* found that, of the 3,007 faith groups which responded to its survey, each group contributed an average of eight social action projects, four paid staff activities, and 66 volunteer roles; if these figures were extrapolated out *only* to the same proportion of the nation's faith communities that responded to the survey, this alone would amount to 213,692 social action projects being run across the faith sector each year.[108] As of 2017, 94% of Anglican churches ran or supported community events, 86% ran an elderly lunch club, 70% ran pastoral initiatives (such as street pastors, befriending or counselling), and 53% ran a community café.[109] In 2019, over 5,600 people attended weekly luncheon clubs and 8,600 people experiencing, or at risk of, homelessness received support through weekly drop-ins run by the Salvation Army.[110] Across the country, this all amounts to vast swathes of sustained engagement – even aside from the significant contribution of other denominations.[111]

The strong networks of relationships which emerge around churches are of value to community cohesion for three main reasons.

First, they are a direct intervention against loneliness and isolation. This is an area of cohesion policy which has received increased attention since the appointment of the first Church leader for Loneliness (since abolished) in 2018. Independent research estimated that as many as 23% of the UK population felt "always or often" lonely even before the pandemic – and while the *Office of National Statistics'* figure is far lower (5%), they also found between April and May 2020 that 31% felt their wellbeing had been affected by feelings of loneliness "in the last 7 days" (what they have termed the "lockdown lonely").[112] Whether in normal time or lockdown, social networks which keep individuals connected and engaged are therefore critical – and where physical gathering is possible, simple coffee mornings are underrated as one of the few opportunities for the community to come together on the basis of nothing other than a desire to connect:

> *Although a church coffee morning might not sound like rocket science... the one in my village has been described as a lifeline...*

Often, that might be the only thing in an area. And also, it's not treating people in silos as "lonely", or 'homeless", or "with mental health problems", or "over 55". It's just an event bringing people together whoever those people are and that's really interesting I think, and really, really rich.' [113]

In Thanet, an area identified by a Co-op British Red Cross Partnership as one of 39 target areas in which to address serious loneliness in 2016,[114] and where many of our participants mentioned they were concerned about social isolation, one participant involved in running a church-based community meal told us their initiative had been a relational lifeline for two users in particular:

> Simple coffee mornings are underrated as one of the few opportunities for the community to come together on the basis of nothing other than a desire to connect.

We must have been going about a year or so, I suppose... We sort of said, "Over Christmas we hope you had a nice time. Tell your friends about us. You can bring your friends to the Christmas party if you want to." And this one couple said "We don't have any friends."... I said, "You must have neighbours?" "Yes, but they're not our friends at all. We don't mix."... Anyway, when they came back after Christmas... one of the other ladies – I think she lives with her dad – and I said, "Did you have a nice time?" and she said "Brilliant" and she'd gone to this couple over Christmas. [115]

The same participant spoke of how one of the regular attenders at another church-run community meal in the area had recently died, and the funeral congregation consisted of three family members, six fellow attenders at the community meal, and twelve members of the local Salvation Army. For that individual – not a member of the church congregation in a strict sense – the local churches had become their primary social network.

Secondly, at a more structural level, strong networks enable stronger joint responses to challenges facing the community. This was strikingly demonstrated by one Salvation Army leader, who told us that the total food bill for their homeless drop-in programme in 2016-17 was just £18 – despite an estimated commercial value of £40,000-£45,000 – because they were regularly given unsold food for free as a result of strong relationships built up with local supermarkets.[116] In this way, a response is amplified by its embeddedness in a wider network.

Relatedly, churches are extremely well positioned to draw on wider Christian networks beyond the local level, giving isolated or under-resourced neighbourhoods access to a vast range of contacts and resources across the nation (and even the world). The most striking example of this phenomenon is the Near Neighbours scheme – a cohesion initiative administrated by the Church Urban Fund and run through the Church of England's parish system. Near Neighbours offers funding and support to grassroots initiatives in both "social action" and "social integration" with the aim of "bringing people together" to "get to know each other better, build relationships of trust, and collaborate together on initiatives that improve the local community they live in".[117] Local coordinators are employed in each area where Near Neighbours runs, and Anglican parish priests act in an advisory capacity to their local funding applicants. The range of funded projects is broad, from a community orchard in the West Midlands, to the Christian-Muslim Forum and its Church-Mosque Twinning scheme. A

2016 evaluation of Near Neighbours prepared by Coventry University reflected that:

> *the critical roles, skills and networks of the local coordinators – who are provided with a useful level of autonomy and have a first-rate understanding of the local area... as well as the interplay between the various national specialists, enhances the significance of the Programme hugely, helping to boost the impact of grants and build sustainable community networks within neighbourhoods.* [118]

In this way, the deployment of a church network in a flagship cohesion scheme has enabled the best of national and local expertise to come together in pursuit of greater social cohesion outcomes. This is not only a practical advantage, but becomes particularly pertinent when considered in light of David Goodhart's influential account of "Anywheres" (who tend to be mobile, and draw their sense of identity from personal achievement) and "Somewheres" (more strongly communitarian, rooting their sense of identity and belonging in attachment to place) as the major emerging tribes in British politics. If the toxicity of our recent political history can be understood in any sense as a "Somewhere backlash" against "Anywhere over-reach", drawing fuel from a broader tussle between local and global values, churches are well-equipped to navigate the tension. [119]

Thirdly, church-based networks can be accessed by other organisations or groups looking to communicate information quickly relating to events and updates in the community. These networks are especially employed in (though not limited to) relations between communities and local police. For example:

The churches have training in ACT – which is Run, Hide, Tell, Stay Safe... They all got the counter-terrorism briefing on what to look for, what to do, and that message then gets cascaded down.[120] (Police Faith Liaison Officer, London)

I was asked to be a member of the Goal Group, which is a kind of a response group set up by the Met Police... Immediately [after] there was any stabbing, information will be prepared by the police. And we would be able to cascade that information down to almost every local church, giving them an explanation as to what happened and what the police were doing and all that. So if there was a shooting on a Saturday morning, by Sunday morning, we were able to send information out. And we were also able to let those churches know that there would be police presence in front of their buildings today, because people wanted to feel reassured.[121] (Pentecostal Church Leader, Croydon)

[Brexit is] something that we are working really closely with our faith leaders on to disseminate messages to our residents... "If you haven't heard from Central Government, here is what you need to do to apply for Settled Status" – that sort of thing. And here's places where you can get support and whatever.[122] (Councillor, Haringey)

One of the things that I talk about a lot within the interfaith communities is the ability of churches and other religious institutions to reach out beyond where the local government can because they're trusted and they have a congregation that goes beyond what we probably have a reach into. So we will, we will try and get some of our messages and services out through those institutions.[123] (Council Officer, Peterborough)

In all these reflections, church networks were able to include the community in policing and governance decisions – not only enabling a faster community response and protecting the wellbeing of those who are directly affected by such decisions, but bolstering local democracy and strong political representation (that is, what the terminology of the government's own definition of community cohesion describes as "people trusting one another and trusting local institutions to act fairly").[124]

It is worth noting that church-based networks are not always attached to the formal structures of either physical buildings or paid clergy. In particular, chaplains deliberately offer spiritual or pastoral care within organisations (e.g. hospitals, prisons, sports clubs, councils, courtrooms, universities) or settings (e.g. town centre, waterways) other than formal churches; they are not always ordained, and can be paid or voluntary.[125] They meet a wide range of people, and their concern is for the spiritual and pastoral wellbeing of the people they encounter. This may manifest as direct support for individuals, or as work within systems and organisations to enact meaningful and equitable change within their frames of reference (for example where higher education chaplains sit on university pastoral committees, as well as more broadly acting as bridges between university institutions and their local faith communities). At heart, as a rural chaplain in Cornwall summarised, "the role of the chaplain is just a network".[126] From a cohesion perspective, chaplains can be an effective resource for holding relationships of trust and influence, asking questions nobody else is asking within institutions, and affirming the value of the community's shared life beyond profit. So too, recent years have seen a rise of Street Pastors, who volunteer from within local churches to patrol the streets at night-time (in teams of men and women) and listen to, engage with and pray for those they meet on the streets. Street

Pastors now operate in over 300 towns across the UK, with a volunteer network of over 20,000 people.[127]

Less positively, one common criticism of church networks' impact on social cohesion relates to the role of church-run schools, which are seen by some as an exclusive network encouraging the segregation of children from a young age. Church schools are just one element of churches' community profile, and they often receive a disproportionate (or even exclusive) focus in cohesion discussions. This is not a report about faith-based education, and the relevant arguments are well-rehearsed elsewhere.[128] Many church traditions are not involved in the administration of schools at all; neither are all churches ideologically in favour of schools with a religious character. That said, when 26% of all primary schools are Anglican and 9% of all secondary schools are Catholic alone (and a smaller number of schools are run by other Christian denominations, such as the Methodist Church), schools with a religious character clearly remain a significant element of some churches' capacity to impact on cohesion.[129]

Church-based networks are not always attached to the formal structures of either physical buildings or paid clergy.

Criticisms usually focus on schools' use of faith-based admissions criteria, rather than the prospect of a church-governed school *per se*. These criticisms refer to the fact that schools with a religious character (more commonly referred to as "faith schools") are permitted to apply faith-based admissions criteria (only) if they are oversubscribed, and while new academies and free schools are required to allocate at least 50% of their places without reference to faith, new faith voluntary aided schools are allowed up to 100% faith-based oversubscription criteria in their admissions.[130]   Considering these criticisms specifically, there is evidence that educational selection criteria of any kind (and indeed, the power of schools to act as their own admissions authorities) tend to favour children in higher socio-economic groupings: this is because better-off parents are more likely to have the "soft" knowledge, skills and resources to navigate what has in many places become a highly competitive admissions landscape. Competition around schools admission also encourages, and is in turn skewed by, residential sorting as wealthier parents move into desirable catchment areas.[131] In this way, faith-based admissions can feed into wider societal inequalities – and the percentage of children on free school meals (FSM) is generally lower at church schools than schools without a religious character (although FSM eligibility itself does not correlate exactly as a measure of poverty; the Catholic Education Service uses the *Income Deprivation Affecting Children Index* instead, which suggests that Catholic schools in fact recruit more pupils living in the most income-deprived areas than the national average for all schools).[132]

So too, while many church schools (and especially Catholic schools) are highly ethnically diverse, church schools taken as a whole are less diverse than their non-faith equivalents. More worrying still, research by the University of Lancaster in 2018 found startlingly that if a white child and a black child applied for a single remaining seat at a church school in London, the black child would be less than half as likely to be admitted.[133]

Of course, the impact of faith-based admissions criteria will depend hugely on the school and the area in which it is situated; in rural areas, for example, there may be less choice to start with (53% of rural primary schools have a religious character) and so admissions criteria may be less vulnerable to exploitation.[134] Nonetheless, the inequalities noted above are clearly a cohesion concern, and it is the central policy of the Methodist Church not to use faith-based admissions criteria (although they are sometimes used, especially where schools are jointly run by the Methodist Church and the Church of England).[135] In 2017, the Archbishop of Canterbury Justin Welby actively discouraged schools from using faith-based admissions criteria. As of the same year, only two thirds of Church of England state secondary schools used faith-based admissions at all, though the figure is higher for Catholic schools.[136] It is also worth noting the example of Oasis Community Learning – a Multi-Academy Trust set up by a Christian registered charity, the Oasis Charitable Trust, which now runs 53 schools across the country and assigns oversubscribed places with no reference to faith.

At the same time, integration of different groups does not ensure a cohesive society on its own – and there is also a cohesion impact attached to the attitude of suspicion towards religion that is often channelled through the 'faith schools debate', leaving some religious communities feeling disproportionately scrutinised. As one rabbi reflected on an interaction he had with an Ofsted inspector:

> To a certain extent, Ofsted in this country, with its attempts to force various things on Jewish Schools, has definitely caused... a backlash... I had an Ofsted inspector ask me once, "When –" ("when" – that's the important word) "when Jewish belief and British values contradict, what takes precedence?" So I said that I don't believe they do – I don't believe they do contradict... So she said, "But when they do, what will you do?" And I'm like "Well, taking your assumption that they do, and I don't believe they do, then of course... British values". And then they said, "So please

can you give me an example?" And I said, "Not really, because the whole point is that they don't!" It was just mad.[137]

This exchange reflects the way in which debates around schools with a religious character (including those run by churches) amplify assumptions that bridging capital is the only route to a cohesive society, while bonding capital is inherently divisive. Yet as has been argued elsewhere, bonding capital is itself crucial to cohesion insofar as it generates feelings of belonging and increases confidence, which in turn encourages positive bridging opportunities. The two are not necessarily opposed, but can be mutually reinforcing – and schools with a religious character can play a part in this positive process if and when they are run sensitively.[138]

Furthermore, we came across various examples of churches engaging creatively with education (whether they were directly involved in running schools or not) to foster positive understandings of faith and belief, as well as various linking or exchange initiatives between faith groups in the context of schools with a religious character.[139] Moreover, the participants involved in school initiatives expressed their motivations in terms of fostering understanding and serving their communities, not spreading a Christian worldview. To this end, a 2011 Department of Education report found that "the approaches used to promote cohesion, monitor effectiveness and involve the broader community do not differ dramatically between faith and non-faith schools", suggesting that schools with a religious character take their responsibilities to their pupils and the cohesiveness of the wider community seriously.[140] A consideration of church schools in particular cannot be detached from this wider landscape.

At best then, Christian involvement in education has the potential to foster feelings of belonging among children of faith – an important facet of any accepting and pluralist society. Abolishing schools with a religious character outright would generate significant cohesion challenges of its own; a better route forward is to continue to work closely, and in a religiously literate fashion, with schools to ensure inclusivity and diversity in admissions.

Moreover, from a cohesion perspective it is also important to note that education is not limited to the school level. In particular, there is a growing recognition that a greater policy focus on (and funding directed towards) further education is required to ensure a variety of routes to success, and indeed continual opportunities to learn later in life, which aid social mobility and promote social cohesion.[141] This wider view on education has been championed by high-profile secular voices such David Goodhart, who has recently stressed the importance of further education.[142] It is also an area that the Free Churches Group itself has worked especially to support: education is one of the three core working areas of the Free Churches Group (alongside healthcare and prisons), and a Free Churches vision statement on further education was produced in 2017, emphasising that FE principles of "diversity, inclusion, empowerment, lifelong learning, and service to all in the local community resonate with Free Church values of openness, justice, freedom, regard for all in the community, and valuing each person as a child of God". [143]

Leadership: churches representing and empowering the community

Turning to our third major church asset, churches are a vital source of community leadership – not only in the form of clergy and paid staff, but also (at best) as champions of personal empowerment and dignity at the grassroots.

First then, formal church leaders can be critical in the representation of local interests, as a visible expression of community solidarity, and as channels of sustained communication between different groups in a local or national community. Above all, participants across all sectors recognised the importance of public faith leadership in times of crisis and challenge. This could be framed in praise of churches, or criticism of others: one councillor in Haringey reflected that he had been particularly impressed with the level of representation and engagement offered by Haringey's faith leaders in recent years, while a church-based participant in the same borough felt the 2011 Tottenham riots could have been averted if the police had listened to church leaders pleading for better police-community engagement after the shooting of Mark Duggan.[144] Meanwhile, in Bolton, faith leaders were able to act quickly and together to gather the community in prayer after the taxi driver Alan Henning (from nearby Eccles) was kidnapped and murdered in Syria in 2014.[145] We also heard of public-facing church/faith and belief responses to terrorist incidents, far-right activism, significant anniversaries, and international humanitarian crises.[146]

Some of our participants reflected that public faith leadership predominantly seemed to emerge when something had happened, and they would like to see more of it in 'normal' time – for example, one councillor in Peterborough suggested that "it's got to be regular... we need to have church leaders having the regular columns in local newspapers, you know, to say this, you know, to, to get that message of unity." [147] There is clearly scope to expand the place of public faith leadership. However, the community responses which already happen could not emerge without well-developed and pre-existing networks of church- and faith-based leadership, which are often active at a personal level (including through formal channels) even in the absence of immediate community concerns. Indeed, in the best examples of public faith leadership that we found, it was once again precisely this quiet work behind the scenes which made such effective response to crisis possible – as is explored further in chapter three.

Less positively, we did hear some criticisms that public faith leadership can replicate divisive or exclusive power dynamics, particularly around gender, given that many faith traditions (including various Christian ones) do not accept women in formal religious leadership. [148] These issues are certainly more acute in formal settings such as interfaith or ecumenical councils; they are also exacerbated where other community organisations limit their faith engagement to the leadership level, rather than engaging with laypeople who might be just as (if not more) willing and able to work outside the confines of the church. Therefore, as one Anglican priest advised:

In the best examples of public faith leadership that we found, it was once again precisely this quiet work behind the scenes which made such effective response to crisis possible.

> *Don't just think that the vicar is representative of all the congregation. What might be more useful is to say, "Would you mind putting this in your newsletter?" or something... When I was working for [a different] diocese, I hardly ever worked with vicars. I nearly always worked with laypeople. And they were so engaged... They did brilliant things.* [149]

Encouraging a wider perspective on church leadership is not without its own challenges – not least because of cultural expectations around the role of clergy. As one churchwarden expressed:

> *People want to see the vicar... And actually even the nice non-stipendiary church leader or self-supporting vicar is second best to a certain – you know, if I go and visit someone because they are poorly, I'm not seen as visiting from the church, and I'll be told nobody from the church has been. And I think "But I'm here!" but I don't have a white strip around my neck.* [150]

Churches cannot and should not rely on their ordained leaders alone, and one concern which particularly arose among those denominations with rotational ministry (i.e. where church leaders move to another area after a certain number of years) was the impact of this system on networks of relationships that had built up between institutional leaders in local areas. Simply, when people move on, relationships have to start again with new faces and new priorities:

> *A church in a community is more than that church in a community. That community is part of the town... So you get a new leader in who says "I'm not interested in homeless people, I'm more interested in evangelism", say. Well, that could be that church being taken away from delivering.* [151]

These concerns must be set against the many occurrences where the rootedness of the church and its congregation were specifically noted – as reflected in the depth of church networks explored above. However, greater flexibility around postings (allowing those leaders who want to stay to do so) for those working in an itinerant system – at least where there is a strong 'fit' between leaders and community – may well foster cohesion benefits, in conjunction with a strong focus on engaging and mobilising the laity where possible.

In sum, those inside *and* outside the church would benefit from adopting a broader view of Christian leadership – and the advantages of paid and formal positions are always most positively felt when balanced with inclusive church structures and systems that encourage the wider engagement of the congregation.

After all, formal representation is only the tip of the iceberg where leadership as a cohesion asset is concerned. A theme that came through strongly across all case studies was the role of churches in supporting grassroots initiatives and building soft skills as a sort of "social training ground" – in other words, as a place where leaders are created.[152] As one participant reflected, now a church church leader in an independent network:

> In one sense I had a leadership role [in previous work as a BBC producer] but in reality, I wasn't a leader. I didn't know how to bring people together. I didn't know how to hold a meeting. I could do it, but I have no real skills in it because I wasn't passionate. And now... I have a passion for people and so I am leading people in English lessons, or leading people in Bible Study, or leading people in a parade... Leading people to get out of their houses.[153]

If leadership is fundamentally about "taking initiative in relationship", [154] a community with more proactive leaders of this kind will have more people taking the initiative required to champion community concerns. This also relates to the cohesion premium associated with individual influencers in a community, and we found that the most impressive community initiatives were often being pushed forward by one or two individuals with a particular passion to see them work (as explored further in the "vision" section below). [155]

Relatedly, an explicit concern for individual empowerment ran through many church-based social initiatives. This was encapsulated in the holistic nature of many church-based community projects. For example, one church-based drop-in service in East Lindsey

> *...started as a bit of a job club and it's sort of expanded. We're now drawing people who are involved with housing as well. Age Concern come along as well, so there are particular issues in that way. And we're looking at working with other groups about addiction and this sort of area.* [156]

66

A concern for dignity and purpose as the basis of a more cohesive society was particularly common among church-based interviewees.

A concern for dignity and purpose as the basis of a more cohesive society was particularly common among church-based interviewees.[157] "Dignity" was mentioned especially frequently among Catholic participants, reflecting its centrality in Catholic Social Teaching and demonstrating how a church's religious concerns can filter into the motivations of individuals across their communities.[158] This again emphasises, as chapter one has argued, that churches are not simply generic community groups. Rather, their positive community role is shaped and defined by an underlying religious commitment. Consequently, as one well-known cohesion academic reflected:

> *I think there's one way [that churches have a positive impact on cohesion] which really has not generally been commented on very much, and that is that just about every faith group constantly promotes positive messages about the respect for other human beings, the need for tolerance, the need for*

understanding. And that's often at a pretty much subliminal level really. It might be, you know, posters on church doors and noticeboards, it might be the messages that the Archbishop of Canterbury gives at some official oration or the Queen's birthday or whatever it is... If you add all of the impacts of these different faith organisations to gather this constant messaging, social messaging, about the virtues of that form of morality, I think is absolutely huge. [159]

At best, this positive messaging starts in the early years, and churches run a significant amount of children's and youth work. Not only do many churches engage with young families and children, but youth groups for older children are particularly common, and can offer important social opportunities which keep teenagers safe and engaged where there are few other outlets in a local area. We also saw more unusual offerings such as developed mentoring opportunities (including through Christian youth charities run separately from local churches) and lobbying on behalf of the youth for concerns that particularly affect them.[160] Many churches are doing extremely important work in this area.

That said, there are limitations to the churches' youth engagement when considered as a whole – not least that, given the drop-off in faith affiliation among younger demographics, many churches are likely to find themselves without the direct links to the youth community that they have traditionally enjoyed. But we also heard criticisms that churches had not always been as proactive and engaged as they might have been on youth-targeted social cohesion issues, and in particular, knife and violent crime. Once again, some churches are doing a lot in this area – and even leaving other church-based assets aside, the simple fact that they have buildings which can be opened as supervised spaces at the end of the school day means they have a lot to offer. However, there were frustrations that the Church has not spoken with a unified voice on youth violence, as well as criticisms that local congregations could be more concerned to bolster their own youth congregations than acting strategically with other churches in the area to provide strong youth ministry – or indeed, to protect the interests of young people in the community.

This has created a "vacuum" by which certain churches (both certain traditions, and individual congregations within a local area) are seen to dominate youth ministry.[161] Not everybody welcomes this dynamic, and over the duration of the Commission particularly concerning accusations have emerged about possible financial exploitation and even abuse of young people by the well-known London-based church SPAC Nation, which came to prominence after stories of ex-gang members laying their weapons at the altar gained positive media attention in 2018. The church has ostensibly enjoyed unrivalled success in drawing young people out of gang culture and youth violence, making these accusations all the more painful for those who view it as a best-practice example. In June 2020, it was announced that the church's lead pastor was stepping down and the church rebranded as NXTION Family, dividing into five separate congregations.[162]

Youth ministry ideally should not fall to certain churches, nor should it be a source of competition between congregations, but is a joint responsibility for everyone in the Church. There is more that can be done. However, there is no doubt that providing strong and effective leadership for young people is something that many churches are well-positioned to offer – and indeed, there are already a wide-range of initiatives ongoing, many of which will never become headline news but are vital for social cohesion within our communities.

Convening power: churches as trusted facilitators

The combination of deep networks and strong leadership gives rise to another distinct cohesion asset in churches: convening power. This is the capacity to hold conversational space, and so to coordinate between disparate parties and interests in pursuit of common solutions – and it can emerge naturally and informally at a grassroots level. As one independent church pastor in Haringey described movingly:

> [Churches] are natural convenors. It's our nature: we congregate. So we get what it takes to bring people out. We are the "called-out-ones" [referencing the literal meaning of the Greek word for "church", "ekklesia"]. Our natural instinct is to reach out. That is the nature of the church: come, I'll make you fishers of men. We are fishers of men... We go out and we fish in the most difficult of situations, because we believe we have a responsibility here.[163]

In Haringey itself, a good example of this organic convening power in action is the London Peace Alliance, which emerged in 2001 directly out of the support of Pray Haringey (an ecumenical network of church leaders praying for the borough) in seeking a more collaborative, creative and comprehensive approach to tackling knife crime in the borough. The Alliance focuses on empowering and mentoring young people to act as positive role models ("ambassadors for peace") to their even younger peers, and runs London Week of Peace which gathers together communities from across London in a week of events and an awards ceremony which recognises best practice examples in the prevention of youth violence. This is an example of church-based convening power at its best and most ambitious, springing organically out of the spiritual life of the churches and in direct pursuit of a more cohesive society.

On a similar theme, the Commission was particularly impressed by the "Ignite" scheme at St Paul's Church, Cliftonville in Thanet – a series of evening café style events attended by many vulnerable adults, as part of which a series of discussions and activities were offered on a range of ethical and spiritual themes. This included topics such as the quality of opportunities for young people in the local area, and how the justice system should work, therefore providing a space where those on the margins of society were brought to the centre and could explicitly discuss the sort of society they wanted to create. In this sense, the church was convening conversations that would otherwise never have happened – bringing together people who would never have mixed – in a rare example of genuine public moral reasoning.

More formally, we found several notable examples of churches being used as a neutral party in liaison and arbitration, especially in times of crisis and particularly where other community stakeholders are seen as divisive – for example, if the police are the focus of criticism, or the politics of an area are particularly marginal.[164] This might be navigated behind the scenes at the level of personal negotiation (here again, the moderator is not necessarily a formal church leader, and chaplains can be particularly valuable as neutral parties in dispute).[165] On a larger and more public scale, it was church representatives who were asked to chair Croydon's community consultation after the riots of 2011:

The reason that we were asked as the churches... to chair the first meeting, was because the convenors at the time had a great relationship with the Chief Executive of Croydon Council, and he couldn't see any other group that he knew who he could trust to run that meeting. [166]

The chair of that meeting was pastor of a Newfrontiers church. So too, the Anglican Bishop of Croydon subsequently chaired the Croydon Opportunity and Fairness Commission, which launched its findings in 2016 – and this hints at the fact that churches' innate convening capacity can be bolstered by the particular cultural significance of the established Church of England.[167] It is worth noting the strong national voices campaigning for both disestablishment and a fully secular system (the National Secular Society and Humanists UK are perhaps the best known). Furthermore, at a local level in our own research, various participants reflected that support for establishment among other faith and belief groups was (often) born out of a pragmatic recognition that Anglicanism was (often) best-placed to represent faith interests in the public sphere, rather than a belief that Anglicans were inherently better placed to do so.[168] In other words, there are natural convenors in other traditions who may come to the foreground if the balance of resources changed at a local and national level. This is neither a criticism of the Church of England, nor an argument against establishment. But it is a recognition that 'convening power' involves just that – power – and is not always straightforward, just as it can be fostered less formally and less obviously in a variety of ways across all ecclesiastical and religious traditions.

We found several notable examples of churches being used as a neutral party in liaison and arbitration.

That said, previous Theos polling exploring attitudes towards the next coronation ceremony suggests that the Church of England remains the religious setting least likely to be viewed as alienating among the general public – and one Anglican vicar strikingly recalled the local mosque erecting a banner welcoming "our Archbishop to Derby" during the Archbishop of Canterbury's recent visit to the city, indicating some sense of shared ownership over Anglican structures in other faith traditions.[169] This bears similarity to the way cathedrals can be perceived by the public as belonging to the whole community – and we spoke to various Anglican leaders, especially in cathedrals, who took their special responsibility for (in the words of one Anglican participant) "holding the common sacred ground" very seriously.[170] For now at least, and at a local level in particular, the concentration of buildings and formal leadership structures within Anglicanism means the Church of England is particularly well-placed to hold convening relationships. As noted in chapter one, an example of the Church of England using this reach positively as a practical asset is through the Near Neighbours scheme – and while some objections have been raised to the use of Anglican structures for a government-funded cohesion initiative, overall engagement with Near Neighbours has been extremely positive: a 2013 assessment by Coventry University found that the scheme was "a truly multi-faith programme, accessible to all faiths and reaching beyond the Christian faith to enable significant amounts of interaction between people of many different faith". [171]

Volunteers: churches as congregations in action

Levels of volunteering are used as a measure of the strength of cohesion in their own right – and the churches'

capacity to raise volunteers was often noted by those outside the church. For example,

> *The one thing that churches have done phenomenally well, which councils have never tapped into is that sense of service, that sense of volunteering service... that sense of social action, that we can, we can change the thing that we want to change. (Council officer, Plymouth)* [172]

> *Regular grassroots is much harder. It does happen. I think it happens perhaps in churches more than anywhere else. I don't know if that's a totally skewed reflection, but I do see that. (Rabbi, Prestwich.)* [173]

Is this a "totally skewed reflection" as the participant above suggests it might be? In short, no – though it's complicated. The *2009-2010 Citizenship Survey* found a difference of just 1% between net levels of volunteering (at least once a year) among Christian respondents and the population at large (though there were larger swings in volunteering commitment between different faith traditions, and only the 'other religion' group volunteered more than Christians). [174] However, these figures do not account for the depth of faith commitment, which does make a difference here: it was noted in chapter one that *frequently practising* Christians are the faith group most likely to volunteer regularly for a local charitable initiative in London – while *non-practising* Christians are the least (61% to 33%, against a London average of 47%).[175] This chimes with 2017 data from Pew Research Centre, which found that 28% of 'high commitment' Christians in Western Europe had spent at least an hour a month participating a charitable or volunteer organisation, compared to just 11% of 'low commitment' Christians' – and 14% of the religiously unaffiliated.[176] The number of respondents who identify as Christian by default is likely to be larger than in the other faith groups, and the impact of non-practising Christian responses on affiliation-based volunteering data is therefore likely to be hiding the true potency of churches in raising volunteers.

Church-generated volunteer capacity is also not always channelled through church-based initiatives. As a charity CEO in Solihull told us:

> *Traditionally a lot of volunteers come through their Christian faith anyway so I can see that there are links when we might not be working... directly with the churches, although we do a bit, we do know that a lot of our volunteers are answering their own call to action kind of thing by volunteering and doing something good.* [177]

Especially in rural areas, churches can also function as a focal point for community activity in a broader sense, and beyond the strict confines of its own congregation. For example, one participant in a rural Cornish village told us:

> *There are certain groups that I don't know if they are actually church or actually village; it becomes blurred. There's the pub quiz which raises a little money for the church... any money that is made goes to the church... but is that a church or a community function? It's certainly full of people that don't go to church. The chap who rings the bells, who organises the bell-ringer... he's not a church goer. The person who puts the appropriate flag up [in the church]... she's not a church person, but she performs these functions. And in fact, the person who unlocks the church is a church goer but not a Sunday by Sunday – not a regular.* [178]

On this point, the churches' capacity not only to raise volunteers but to *coordinate* them should not be underestimated. As demonstrated by the hundreds of thousands of people who signed up to the 'army' of NHS volunteer responders early in lockdown and were never called upon for work, organisational capacity and the coordination of volunteers can be as critical in generating broad civic engagement as the good will of the volunteers themselves; the organisational assets which churches bring (for example, in setting rotas, ensuring accountability, and avoiding doubling-up) are themselves necessary to convert good will into action. [179] Again, this is one sense in which the churches offer grassroots and implicit convening power as a community resource.

Nonetheless, raising volunteers is not without its own challenge for churches, and it is only likely to become harder as congregations shrink and grow older:

> *I think, like a lot of areas, the church is shrinking, so there's great ambition but not much potential to do stuff... I've certainly seen that where... you know, it's a Methodist Church that's being run by maybe 5 or 6 people aged over 70. They just haven't got the capacity to keep doing things.* [180]

This reflects the disparity between perceptions of churches' capacity, and the reality that most congregations are small: the median average weekly attendance at an Anglican church is just 32 people.[181] That churches so successfully generate volunteers when only around 11% of the UK population actually attend a worship service even once a month points to the fact that the churches' volunteer base is not just a practical benefit, but the outworking of a further asset: vision. [182]

Vision: "I felt God asking me a question"

A vision for change and transformation is perhaps the most important – certainly the most unifying – of the churches' cohesion assets: that is, the vision to love one's neighbours more fully, to see potential in the community (and the Church) where others have not, or where hope and pride in a community is waning, and to commit to a process of personal and communal transformation. As one Baptist church leader said of an extremely deprived estate within Solihull local authority, "How do we show Christ here? You know, I think this is one of God's favourite places. No offence to anywhere else, but it is." [183] To this end, many church-based participants in communities that were otherwise viewed as "left behind" saw it as central to their role to imbue a sense of hope and pride in place – often linking the hope in God they had as Christians with a sense of positive drive for their neighbourhoods. [184]

Of course, it goes without saying that churches are not the only organisations with positive vision for their communities. Both Bolton and Plymouth were benefiting from significant secular "vision" campaigns – and indeed, support for the Bolton 2030 Vision from the local churches was particularly striking, as we shall see in chapter three. Nonetheless, we can at least say that the extent of churches' contribution to social cohesion is largely determined by the extent of their vision – and in this sense, while vision can be underrated (and perhaps even deliberately ignored) as 'the religious bit' of their mission, it shapes and colours everything which is distinctive about their community contribution.

In a church context, some participants spoke about vision generated specifically by formal church leaders, as institutional guarantors of community vision. This can be particularly vital in rural communities where, as above, the church often becomes a focal point for community activity:

> I think that's sometimes the role of the church leader... to do the setting the vision. [In] the Deanery we've got one of the parishes where we've got a really good priest... their job was to sort of get the community together, sort of be the link person, be that sort of community connector. (Anglican Area Dean, rural ministry expert.) [185]

Such vision can manifest simply as a faith-led desire to serve the wider community, and especially as the vision to see areas of need that are not being effectively tackled by other means. Examples of this sort are everywhere, but one particularly striking example is the number and type of church-led responses to holiday hunger (whereby families struggle to feed their children during school holidays, when term-time entitlement to free school meals is suspended and childcare costs rise to cover the additional unsupervised time). Local churches are heavily involved in this area (a startling 52% of Anglican churches run initiatives in some way related to holiday or breakfast provision, or after school clubs),[186] and Christian children's charities often help to coordinate local efforts. For example, the Bradford-based charity Transforming Lives for Good (TLG) coordinates local church efforts as part of its "Make Lunch" initiative, which supports churches to provide hot meals for children in struggling families in their own settings. Since the scheme began, TLG's partner churches have distributed over 120,000 meals in more than 100 locations across the UK, in addition to providing a support network of relationships for the families of these children.[187] One council officer in Plymouth praised their local churches' work on holiday hunger:

[It's] amazing. Absolutely amazing. It's ground-breaking stuff, and it's given us the freedom as a local authority to do more... They really were the instigators of it, to a degree. Now they're very much in partnership with us to the point where we don't want any children to go hungry in the city in the summer. [188]

This sort of vision – seeing a problem that others are struggling to solve, and working to find a solution – is a good example of how asset- and needs-based approaches should best inform one another: once again, deployment of church assets is most effective where churches also have a strong perception of their communities' needs.

For a striking number of our Christian participants "vision" sprang more personally out of a literal sense of God's leading.

For a striking number of our Christian participants, however, "vision" of the need around them was not felt to have emerged out of institutionally led problem-solving – nor even any sort of human calculation at all. Rather, it sprang more personally out of a literal sense of God's leading:

I wanted God to provide me with a group to go to, and I kept feeling him say, "No, I want you to start one". I was like "No!" Anyway, I did start The Challenge group in the end, and it's a playgroup and support group for anyone who's got a baby or young child with disabilities. [189]

We were still wondering what else we could do, and I was praying and the only word I could get was "Storehouse". And it kept coming back and back and back. And I thought the only thing I can think of with "Storehouse" is food... I had a chat with Bob, and I said, "I think we should start a foodbank". [190]

I remember something of a spiritual experience for me, during a prayer time, when I felt God ask me a question. Or a question popped up in my mind: whether it was God asking me or me just thinking it, it was a very strange question, and it was "Are you ready to pastor people that will never come to your church?" [191]

These reflections describe personal experiences of finding direction through one's personal spiritual life, and point to the under-appreciated role of prayer in faith-based social action, as the directing force behind much of what Christians offer in their communities. Many participants emphasised the need for champions who took on causes and pushed vision through, as noted in the leadership section, and this can often be the result of this sort of personal leading.[192] Therefore, secular organisations should not be intimidated or put off by such overtly Christian framing: a powerful spiritual vision is the engine of churches' presence in their communities, not a problem to be overcome before the church can act as a suitable partner.

After all, initiatives are much harder to sustain where this initial powerful vision gets lost or becomes unclear. This can often occur when a key person moves on, or can no longer cope with the scale of the work:

So up until the end of the last academic year there was an event called [Anon.] that was like a youth event... And over the years that sort of dwindled in support, the vision got unclear and it basically got landed with one particular person. It just became not viable basically. [193]

Various participants emphasised that projects worked most effectively when they drew on the vision and passion of the congregation, and what they would support.[194] Likewise, where churches are less engaged in the community, it is often at root because of a lack of vision. In some cases, participants were quite critical of unfulfilled potential where churches just didn't see a need to engage beyond their congregation. A Methodist chaplain in Bolton reflected that some churches were certainly better at engaging than others:

> *Some... buy into the vison of Christian community cohesion. Some just won't get it at all, because their focus is trying to keep their roof over their head, trying to maintain their own building, their own space, and I think that, you know, trying to get a broader vison is harder... it's not just a financial challenge; it's a lack of vision, and a lack of understanding. And a lack of recognition that actually it is a Christian obligation to be part and parcel of the town that you live in.* [195]

At the other extreme, churches can be extremely motivated and outward-facing, but may not frame their engagement in terms of seeking a more cohesive society *per se*. Often churches are primarily concerned to address extreme material need in their community engagement, and some participants reflected on their own experience that they felt more comfortable talking about "social justice" or "social action" than "social cohesion".[196] This is not a problem in itself, but may become problematic if no attempt is made to repair the social inequality resulting from (or perhaps underlying) the need being addressed. This relates to wider concerns around class dynamics within the Church, and several participants reflected critically that Christians could be more comfortable in taking on the powerful role of a "helper" rather than being open to true relationship with those of a different socio-economic status. Of course, this becomes more contentious where there are significant economic extremes in an area – that is, where inequalities are more divisive. That said, this criticism should be viewed in a wider context: as seen throughout this report, churches do run vast numbers of initiatives where relationship is the explicit aim: coffee mornings, community festivals, elderly lunch clubs, youth clubs, and so on. Viewing these initiatives as an important social witness in their own right, rather than as nice-to-haves, leads to a more accurate recognition of the church's (sometimes implicit) concern for social cohesion, even beyond the more obvious 'acts of mercy'.

More negatively, elements of some churches' vision can be controversial in society at large, and therefore damaging to community trust in churches. Important areas of concern in this regard are church teachings on sexuality and gender – above all, the teaching of some churches on homosexuality, and their position on women in leadership. Those observing the churches from the outside should recognise that there is a diversity of Christian positions on these issues – as one participant reflected, same-sex marriage is the "Church of England's Brexit; it's close to irreconcilable".[197] It is also worth noting that issues around sexuality and gender came up less in interviews than expected – almost always as a general reflection on the Church as a whole, rather than individual churches in specific communities, and more so in the form of frustrations from church-based participants than the concerns of those outside (again, with small numbers in either case). Several interview participants who expressed conservative sentiments on sexuality and gender issues also expressed the passionate desire – supported by action, often over many years – to enrich and serve their whole communities, and were keen to stress their concern for the community. Nonetheless, it clearly does affect perceptions of the Church, both from within and without, and in this sense can limit their capacity to engage more generally.

Conclusion

This chapter has considered the assets churches deploy to foster social cohesion, as a way of assessing the extent of their impact on communities across England.

Some aspects of the churches' community profile can be controversial or even divisive – the main two issues here being church-run schools and some churches' teachings on issues around sexuality and gender. However, the impact of these issues on cohesion itself is often inflated in the public imagination. Of course, church-run schools should work within their communities and alongside the relevant authorities to make their admissions policies as inclusive as possible, but their existence is not itself inherently damaging to cohesive societies. Issues around sexuality and gender, while important in their own right, were mentioned less than might be expected in the specific context of the churches' impact on social cohesion. Church assets (above all, expensive buildings) can also be experienced as a distraction or a burden by their congregations, leading to unfulfilled potential where community engagement is concerned. And there are certainly issues on which churches as a whole could be working more concertedly and connectedly together: we have noted that there is more that many churches could be doing to respond to youth violence especially.

Nonetheless, the overall picture of the churches' impact on social cohesion is an overwhelmingly positive one: where churches have a realistic understanding of their resources and are using them to their full potential, they not only offer an unrivalled source of physical capital scattered equally throughout the country; so too, they act as the social capillaries of their communities, offering a wellspring of natural and formal leadership, convening difficult conversations between different groups, motivating individual members of their congregations to give back, and seeing (and enacting) the full potential of their communities where others do not. Much of this good work is already happening, and a better understanding of these vital assets would enable a more concerted use of them in pursuit of a more cohesive society.

This quiet and concerted love of neighbour is emblematic of a cohesion approach that looks beyond the next crisis. The discussion has also particularly uncovered how often the line between bonding and bridging is blurred: time and again, the churches demonstrate how both can be fostered alongside one another, as well as how one can lead to another. So too, churches illustrate the positive cohesion impact of strong bonding capital itself – too often compared negatively to bridging capital. On all these points, policymakers would do well to take note of the churches' lead.

That said, those churches with the greatest impact are rarely working in isolation. Networks are only a community asset insofar as they enable communication and collaboration; buildings are only effective as gathering sites insofar as people gather in them; leaders are only effective community champions insofar as they bring others along on the journey. In short, a truly cohesive community does not work in silos. Therefore, having outlined some of the ways in which churches contribute to social cohesion on their own terms, the final chapter of this report will consider the place of churches in the wider nexus of community relationships, to evaluate how effectively they work alongside other key groups in the community in the pursuit of greater social cohesion.

[66] Non-church #146, Non-church #157, Non-church #270-1. For a critique of asset-based community development precisely along these lines, see M. A. MacLeod and A. Emejulu, 'Neoliberalism With a Community Face? A Critical Analysis of Asset-Based Community Development in Scotland', *Journal of Community Practice*, 22:4, (2014), pp. 430-450.

[67] Church #48.

[68] Church #173.

[69] For example, Church #57, Non-church #62, Non-church #130, Non-church #196, Church #245, Church #49, Church #274, Non-church #157.

[70] APPG Social Integration, *Healing the Generational Divide* (2019), p. 19; K. Robinson and R. Sheldon, 'Witnessing Loss in the Everyday: Community Buildings in Austerity Britain', *The Sociological Review*, 67:1 (2019), p. 111-125. core.ac.uk/download/pdf/199197053. pdf; Joseph Rowntree Foundation, *The cost of the cuts*, p. 16.

[71] Onward, *Repairing our social fabric*, p. 14.

[72] Non-church #128.

[73] Church #20.

[74] Brierley Consultancy, *UK Church Statistics no. 3*, p. 1.

[75] G. Allport, *The Nature of Prejudice* (Reading, MA.: Addison-Wesley, 1954); M. Hewstone and R. Brown, 'An Integrative Theory of Intergroup Contact', M. P. Zanna (ed.), *Advances in experimental social psychology*, 37 (London: Elsevier, 2005), pp. 255-343.

[76] Church #58.

[77] National Churches Trust, *State of the churches: the impact of Covid-19* (London: NCT, 2020), p. 1. https://www.nationalchurchestrust. org/sites/default/files/29-05-20%20State%20of%20the%20 churches%20COVID-19%20FINAL%20PDF.pdf

[78] Ibid.

[79] Church #188, Church #272, Church #279.

[80] Church #274.

[81] Church #132.

[82] Esp. Church #48, Church #52, Non-church #56; G. Meadows, 'Middlesbrough charities forced to find a new home after centre closure', *The Northern Echo*, 19 February 2020. www.thenorthernecho.co.uk/news/18247127. middlesbrough-charities-forced-find-new-home-centre-closure/

[83] Church #42, Church #330.

[84] Church #326.

[85] Church #300.

[86] Church #295.

[87] Church #141.

[88] Non-church #1.

[89] Church #261.

[90] R. O'Brien and A. Potter-Collins, *2011 Census Analysis: Ethnicity and Religion of the Non-UK Born Population in England and Wales*, (London: *Office for National Statistics*, 18 June2015) www.ons.gov.uk/peoplepopulationandcommunity/culturalidentity/ethnicity/articles/2011censusanalysisethnicityandreligionofthenonukbornpopulationinenglandandwales/2015-06-18

[91] Church #341.

[92] Brierley Consultancy, *UK Church Statistics no. 3*, p. 5.

[93] Church #2, Church #126, Church #130, Church #131, Church #343, Church #346-349, Church #120.

[94] For an example of a policy that reflects these tensions, see *The Diocese of London*, 'The use of church halls by other churches and Christian groups', The Diocese of London www.london.anglican.org/kb/church-hall-use-by-other-churches/

[95] Church #319.

[96] P. Bickley, *People, Place and Purpose* (London: Theos, 2018), p. 77.

[97] Church #290.

[98] Church #161, Church #312.

[99] Non-church #32.

[100] For example, Non-church #200, Non-church #202, Non-church #203, Non-church #264, Non-church #234.

[101] Theos and the Grubb Institute, *Spiritual Capital: The Present and Future of English Cathedrals* (London: Theos, 2012), p. 44. www.theosthinktank.co.uk/cmsfiles/archive/files/Polling/Cathedrals%20Final%20Data%20PDF.pdf See also F. Davis, E. Paulhaus and A. Bradstock, *Moral but no Compass: Government, Church and the Future of Welfare* (Stockport: Rejoice Publications, 2008), p. 65-9.

[102] Non-church #238.

[103] Church #129.

[104] Church #215, Church #84-5, Church #97.

[105] Church #108, see also Church #340, Church #171, Church #108, Church #182.

[106] Non-church #112, Church #92, Church #117, Church #219, Church #206.

[107] The Church of England, 'General Synod votes to apologise over racism', *The Church of England News*, 11 February 2020. www.churchofengland.org/more/media-centre/news/general-synod-votes-apologise-over-racism

[108] Cinnamon Network, *Cinnamon Faith Action Audit* (London: Cinnamon, 2016), p. 7.

[109] Church Urban Fund, *Church in Action: A National Survey* (2017), p. 8.

[110] The Salvation Army, *The Power of Love: How the Salvation Army Changed Lives, 2018* (London: Salvation Army, 2018), p. 2.

[111] It is worth noting that data which are comparably comprehensive to the Anglican Church in Action Survey do not exist in other denominations, and this sort of audit would be welcome for church traditions hoping to assess the scale of their impact on their communities more accurately.

[112] B. DiJulio, L. Hamel, C Muñana, and M. Brodie, 'Loneliness and *Social Isolation* in the *United States*, the *United Kingdom*, and *Japan*: An *International Survey*', *Kaiser Family Foundation, 30 August 2018*. www.kff.org/other/report/loneliness-and-social-isolation-in-the-united-states-the-united-kingdom-and-japan-an-international-survey/

[113] Church #298.

[114] *The Co-operative,* 'Lonely Life Stages: New Study Reveals Triggers for Loneliness Epidemic in the UK', The Co-operative, 8 December 2016 www.co-operative.coop/media/news-releases/lonely-life-stages-new-study-reveals-triggers-for-loneliness-epidemic-in-the-UK

[115] Church #64.

[116] Church #132.

[117] *Near Neighbours,* 'About us', Near Neighbours, 2019 www.near-neighbours.org.uk/about

[118] Centre for Trust, Peace and Social Relations, 'An Evaluative Framework for Near Neighbours' (Coventry: CTPSR, 2016), p. 3. static1.squarespace.com/static/5a68889a90bade540b4da177/t/5b23930603ce64eefd252ea6/1529058057358/An+Evaluation+Framework+for+Near+Neighbours+Report.pdf

[119] D. Goodhart, *The Road to Somewhere: The New Tribes Shaping British Politics* (London: Penguin, 2017), p. 5-7.

[120] Non-church #104.

[121] Church #126.

[122] Non-church #114.

[123] Non-church #200.

[124] Department for Communities and Local Government, *The Government's Response to the Commission on Integration and Cohesion* (London: Crown, 2007), 10.

[125] B. Ryan, *Chaplaincy: A very modern ministry* (London: Theos, 2015), p. 10-16.

[126] Church #293.

[127] Street Pastors, 'About Us'. www.streetpastors.org/about-us-1/

[128] For example, E. Oldfield, E. Bailey and L. Hartnett, *More than an Educated Guess* (London: Theos, 2013); S. Perfect, *Bridging the Gap* (London: Theos, 2020), p. 72-74; Pennington, *Cohesive Societies*, p. 21-23; R. Berkeley, *Right to Divide?: Faith Schools and Community Cohesion* (London: Runnymede Trust, 2008); J. Van den Brande, J. Hillary, and C. Cullinane, Selective Comprehensives: *Great Britain. Access to Top Performing Schools for Disadvantaged Pupils in Scotland, Wales and England* (London: National Foundation for Educational Research and the Sutton Trust, 2019), p. 6.

[129] R. Long and S. Danechi, *Faith Schools in England: FAQs* (London: House of Commons, 2019), p. 17.

[130] Ibid. 6.

[131] Esp. R. Montacute and C. Cullinane, *Parent power 2018* (London: The Sutton Trust, 2018), p. 11-12; but see also The Accord Coalition, *Databank of Independent Evidence on Faith Schools* (London: Accord Coalition, 2020). accordcoalition.org.uk/wp-content/uploads/2013/12/Databank-of-Independent-Evidence-on-Faith-Schools-April-2014.pdf

[132] F. E. S. Montemaggi et al., *The Take-Up of Free School Meals in Catholic Schools in England and Wales* (London: St Mary's University, Twickenham, 2017), p. 7-8, 15. www.stmarys.ac.uk/research/centres/benedict-xvi/docs/free-school-meal-report.pdf

[133] M. Weldon, Secondary School Choice and Selection: National Preferences Data (Lancaster: Department of Education and University of Lancaster, 2018), p. 8. assets.publishing.service.gov.uk/government/uploads/system/uploads/attachment_data/file/732881/Secondary_school_choice_and_selection.pdf

[134] National Secular Society, *The choice delusion* (London: NSS, 2018), p. 5. www.secularism.org.uk/uploads/the-choice-delusion-how-faith-schools-restrict-primary-school-choice-in-england.pdf

[135] *Methodist Education Commission*, 'Education Commission Report', Methodist Education Commission, 2012. www.methodistschools.org.uk/downloads/policies-on-website-/conf-education-commission-report-030712.pdf

[136] J. Harman, *No Room at the Inn: Exclusive admissions policies in Church of England secondary schools* (London: Humanists UK, 2017), p. 4. humanism.org.uk/wp-content/uploads/2017-12-18-LW-v6-FINAL-No-Room-At-The-Inn.pdf

[137] Non-church #144.

[138] Pennington, *Cohesive Societies: Faith and Belief*, p. 28-9, 45-51, 61-62.

[139] Church #92, Church #134, Church #137, Church #210, Church #234, Church #247, Church #267, Church #283.

[140] Department for Education, *Community cohesion and PREVENT: How have schools responded?* (London: Department for Education, 2011), p. 11, 35-36.

[141] Further education refers to educational choices made after secondary level (16+) but below degree level.

[142] D. Goodhart, *The Road to Somewhere*, p. 33-37, 147-178; D. Goodhart, *Head Hand Heart: The Struggle for Dignity and Status in the 21st Century* (London: Penguin, 2020).

[143] G. Handscomb, J. Wise and S. Iles, *Serving the Marginalised: Free Churches vision and policy for Further Education* (London: Free Churches Directors' Group, 2017), p. 3-5. static1.squarespace.com/static/58359f279de4bbe7aba10e31/t/5adef5896d2a730adc012c23/1524561290585/Education+-+Visi on+Statement+FE+Serving+the+Marginalised+-+2017.pdf

[144] Church #108, Non-church #114.

[145] Non-church #10.

[146] Non-church #10, Non-church #15, Non-church #24, Church #193, Church #197, Non-church #200, Non-church #202, Church #278, Non-church #258, Church #135, Non-church #160, Non-church #266.

[147] Non-church #191.

[148] Non-church #12, Church #221.

[149] Church #222.

[150] Church #292.

[151] Church #13.

[152] Non-church #130.

[153] Church #4.

[154] G. Lakey, 'Powerful Beyond Measure: Trusting the Call to Leadership', *Philadelphia Yearly Meeting*, 4 February 2016, 17:45. www.youtube.com/watch?v=Kum9RVqOo_s

[155] See below, pp. 102-7; Church #352, Non-church #195, Non-church #12, Non-church #275, Non-church #40, Church #48, Church #117, Non-church #177.

[156] Church #322.

[157] Church #57, Church #116, Church #219, Non-church #182, Church #88, Church #136, Church #317.

[158] For example, "The Church is an expert in humanity, and anticipating with trust and with active involvement she continues to look towards the 'new heavens' and the 'new earth' (2 Peter 3:13), which she indicates to every person, in order to help people to live their lives in the dimension of authentic meaning. *'Gloria Dei vivens homo'*: the human person who fully lives his or her dignity gives glory to God, who has given this dignity to men and women."

Pontifical Council for Justice and Peace, *Compendium of the Social Doctrine of the Church* www.vatican.va/roman_curia/pontifical_councils/justpeace/ documents/rc_pc_justpeace_doc_20060526_compendio-dott-soc_en.html

[159] Non-church #360.

[160] Church #131, Church #106.

[161] Church #137.

[162] B. Bryant, 'SPAC Nation: Church "financially exploited members"', *BBC News,* 16 December 2019. www.bbc.co.uk/news/uk-england-london-50815142; *BBC News,* 'SPAC Nation: MP Steve Reed urges Met Police to reopen criminal inquiry', BBC News, 13 February 2020. www.bbc.co.uk/news/uk-england-london-51478774; 'Santiago-Perez', *Twitter,* 12 June 2020 twitter.com/Gabz_Amadi/status/1271454072105820163 >

[163] Church #121.

[164] Church #126.

[165] See, for example, Rev. J. Herbert, 'Illegal grazing', *Together for the Common Good,* 2020. togetherforthecommongood.co.uk/stories/illegal-grazing

[166] Church #133.

[167] Croydon Opportunity and Fairness Commission, *A Better Croydon For Everyone* (London, 2015). www.croydon.gov.uk/sites/default/files/articles/downloads/ Croydon_Opportunity_%26_fairness%20Commission_final_report.pdf

[168] Church #222, Non-church #238, Church #274, Church #343, Church #252, Non-church #356, Non-church #162.

[169] Church #232; N. Spencer and N. Dixon, *Who wants a Christian coronation?* (London: Theos, 2015), p. 7.

[170] See above, p. 72; Church #194.

[171] T. O'Toole, D. Nilsson DeHanas, T. Modood, N. Meer & S. Jones, *Taking Part: Muslim Participation in Contemporary Governance* (Bristol: Centre for the Study of Ethnicity & Citizenship, 2013), p. 47-48; P. Lewis and C. Dando, 'The Interfaith Movement', *Temple Tracts,* 5:1 (Chester: William Temple Foundation, 2015), p. 9-10; Centre for Trust, Peace and Social Relations, *An Evaluative Framework...Pennington, Cohesive Societies,* p. 36-38.

[172] Non-church #174.

[173] Non-church #144.

[174] Ministry of Communities and Local Government, *Community Life Survey 2009-10* (London: Department for Communities and Local Government, 2010), p. 36. webarchive.nationalarchives.gov.uk/20120919151616/http:/ www.communities.gov.uk/documents/statistics/pdf/164191.pdf

[175] P. Bickley and N. Mladin, *Religious London,* p. 55.

[176] *Pew Research Centre,* '6. Religion and Society', Pew Research Centre, 29 May 2018, www.pewforum.org/2018/05/29/religion-and-society/

[177] Non-church #272.

[178] Church #292.

[179] B. Gardner, 'NHS volunteer army of 750,000 has been given fewer than 20,000 tasks, data reveals', *The Telegraph,* 16 April 2020, www.telegraph.co.uk/news/2020/04/16/least730000-volunteers-nhs-scheme-yet-deployed-care-home-bosses/

[180] Church #290.

[181] The Church of England Research & Statistics Team, *Statistics for Mission 2018,* (London: Church of England Research and Statistics, 2019) www.churchofengland.org/sites/default/files/2019-10/2018StatisticsForMission_0.pdf

[182] See Theos/YouGov, *Spirituality and COVID (YouGov,*2020) docs.cdn.yougov.com/o93kio300s/YG-Archive-11082020-TheosSpirituality.pdf

[183] Church #286.

[184] Church #187, Church #322, Church #13, Church #281.

[185] Church #352.

[186] CUF, *Church in Action,* p. 8.

[187] Church #359; Transforming Lives for Good, *Make Lunch,* www.tlg.org.uk/your-church/make-lunch

[188] Non-church #174.

[189] Church #109.

[190] Church #77.

[191] Church #121.

[192] See above, 91.

[193] Church #166.

[194] Church #48, Church #302, Church #222, Church #245.

[195] Church #28. See also Church #133, Church #165, Church #167, Church #190, Church #178, Church #274.

[196] For example, Non-church #145, Church #147, Church #148, Church #308, Church #57.

[197] Church #193.

3

The Church and other organisations

Cohesive societies necessarily function beyond the strength of individual efforts, but how effectively do churches work with other community organisations to maximise their impact in support of strong cohesion outcomes? How effectively do other organisations engage with churches?

> **"**
> ──────────────
>
> The existing community presence of churches and other faith and belief groups can provide the framework for impromptu shows of community solidarity.

And how effectively are the inherent cohesion benefits of strong working relationships being realised? In the final chapter of this report, churches' relationships with other groups are assessed through three case studies – interfaith engagement, ecumenical engagement, and council-church relationships – which together demonstrate the opportunities of working in collaboration, as well as some of the distinctive issues encountered in different types of collaboration.

Interfaith engagement

Interfaith engagement is by no means the only area in which churches work beyond themselves, but it is perhaps the most obvious to those outside the faith sector. Interfaith working is explicitly concerned with generating bridging opportunities between community groups; in turn, such opportunities have the potential directly to alleviate cohesion tensions and nourish genuine friendships when sustained over time.

Sometimes interfaith engagement happens organically, without a pre-planned interfaith initiative driving it. In these cases, the existing community presence of churches and other faith and belief groups can provide the framework for impromptu shows of community solidarity. For example, one Solihull-based participant (who was herself strongly involved in the town's Faiths Forum) recalled that after the Sri Lanka church shooting, "the Muslims who meet in the community centre actually came to St Alphege's and St Augustine's on Sunday to say 'we are standing in solidarity with you'".[198] So too, a cathedral-based participant told us that, following an arson attack at Peterborough Cathedral in 2001, it was the mosque that sent the first cheque "as a gesture of support knowing that our building was important to us and also to the city". [199] Interactions of this kind happen between faith groups on a piecemeal level all the time, and do not require a formal interfaith council or intentional cohesion scheme. Simply, church structures act in this way as the conduit for steps towards a more cohesive and peaceful future.

That said, formal interfaith work is often the most active and sustained channel for communication between faiths. In previous reports, formal faith forums (and especially interfaith initiatives) have sometimes been criticised for engaging only those who are already convinced of the need to communicate across difference. [200] There is clearly scope for expanding interfaith work and engaging the grassroots further, although it is worth noting that interfaith work in the UK has already expanded and diversified in recent years. It can be initiated by a single faith, several faiths together, or indeed a third party (such as a council or through government funding) – but direct involvement from faith groups themselves is increasingly common. [201]

A particular task might form the heart of the engagement, for example where people of different faiths come together to cook a shared meal, pick litter, or lobby on behalf of a shared political concern. Focusing on a shared task can establish a spirit of equality in bridging relationships, rather than one party feeling like the initiator or helper throughout. It also moves the focus away from worship, and allows the relationship to grow firmly outside a theological setting. This is not only helpful to enable the engagement of those who feel uncomfortable or unwilling to worship alongside those of different faiths; one rabbi also told us he felt that Christian-initiated interfaith work could sometimes be too focused on theology, and therefore could feel like it was intended to help Christians make sense of their *own* relationship to Judaism rather than forging genuine and equal relationships. [202] Many of our participants therefore advised that task-based mixing had been the most effective way of working beyond their own in-groups. [203]

However, task-based engagement doesn't work in isolation: sustained dialogue and long-term strategic planning is also important to ensure the coordination needed to plan new tasks, give a longer afterlife to shared endeavours, and provide space for the trickier conversations. For example, interfaith relations in Bolton particularly benefitted from having a council-funded part-time Interfaith Officer and Interfaith Council (as well as various intra-faith councils) which enabled the coordination of a plethora of practical initiatives, from "Faith Trails" (visiting local faith buildings) and community festivals, to an extremely positive "Passport for Faith" event whereby local schoolchildren met and could ask questions of members of local faith traditions to collect stamps for their "Interfaith Passport". Therefore, the richness of the Bolton interfaith landscape – including task-based work – has been enabled by well-funded and longstanding efforts from all parties. As noted in the recent *Cohesive Societies: Faith and Belief* review, this funding structure was recently adjusted to place a greater focus on funding specific events and outputs, and it is too early to tell what effect that will have on faith relations in the town. [204] However, it is clear that support for interfaith relations goes far beyond measurable or concrete outputs: at their heart, interfaith initiatives are always about investing in relationships.

> *We don't do something because it's a tick-box. It's not about tick-box. We have to make a difference, and it's a slow process. It takes time. It's a drip process... [The interfaith role] is quite a wonderful platform in which people can come together, because they know it is not for money, because I strongly do believe money doesn't answer everything. It may help to pay bills, it may help to – but it's not the answer. The answer has got to be in the things we share.* [205]

By valuing dialogue highly and maintaining a broad focus, the faith sector in Bolton is also well-prepared to deal with crises when they arise – as mentioned in chapter two – and yet, crucially, their approach is not defined by it.

An example of a particularly positive scheme at the grassroots level is "Faithful Friends", running in Forest Gate, Newham – a highly diverse London borough, which in the 2011 census recorded the lowest proportion (9.5%) of residents with no religious affiliation in the country.[206] In such an unusually religious community, Faithful Friends was founded in 2007 to "[promote] friendship and cooperation between Christians, Muslims, Sikhs, Hindus, Jews, and all other faiths in Forest Gate" and to "try and tackle problems in the community that are universal". [207] It is coordinated by the community priest of Emmanuel Church, and was identified by participants from the church, other faith groups, the police, and the public sector as a positive space for sharing and relationship-building between groups. [208] In this way, interfaith communication can serve as its own network across the community – or more accurately, a network of networks – and provides an invaluable framework for those looking to build a more cohesive society.

It must be said that this sort of enthusiasm for interfaith work varies hugely within churches, and there are plenty of churches in which interfaith engagement is almost entirely absent, or even rejected on principle. Often Christians are just not that interested; within communities and even within individual congregations, interfaith work is often sustained by already-engaged champions rather than the church as a whole. In both Prestwich and Peterborough, we found that the same particular churches, led by particularly interfaith-focused vicars, would be mentioned again and again as hubs of local interfaith dialogue. As one of these vicars described:

> There are so many... Christians and I have to say, clergy as well, who couldn't see the point of doing [interfaith discussions]. There might be a fearfulness about, "What if they ask me a question and I couldn't answer?" But there might also be puzzlement about, "Well why would we need to talk about our religion to Muslims? They've got their religion, that's it, and that's not we're called... We're called in the Great Commission to share the good news and the love of Jesus Christ." The other question I'm asked a fair bit is... "Are you trying to convert them?" And I always answer by saying that's not my role. It's the role of the Holy Spirit to do conversion. [209]

Of course, a lack of interest can cut both ways, and churches are not alone in struggling to engage members of their congregations in interfaith efforts. [210] Tellingly, one

Baha'i member involved in local interfaith work in Thanet observed that "when it's [one tradition's] turn to give a talk about their faith, a lot of people turn up. But the next talk that isn't about them, nobody comes. This is a real problem." [211] Therefore, the common criticism that interfaith tends to engage the 'usual suspects' is broadly fair. However, this criticism has sometimes been understood to undermine the efficacy of interfaith work as a whole, and this is less justified: as we have seen, even though there is huge scope to expand the interfaith sector in the UK, the good work which is already happening is hugely enriching for local communities, and often nourishes strategically and communally important relationships that would soon be noticed if they disappeared.

Ecumenical networks

Churches themselves are not all the same, and the range of church traditions in England – particularly in urban areas – is growing. This variety, even within Christianity, can foster a unique cohesion dynamic:

> In Haringey, we have lots of churches. We lost count. At some point, we knew there were at least 200 to 250 churches in Haringey. Because of the diversity of the people coming in, it's a real issue trying to – I mean, I see churches as really at the forefront of community cohesion because the church community is generally speaking multi-ethnic but mono-cultural... and therefore... it's a fantastic place to build understanding and empathy and compassion for all ethnic groups. [212]

Once again, neat distinctions between bonding and bridging capital break down. Firstly, what many assume to be a single faith (i.e. Christianity) is in fact a diverse spectrum of different groups, so that mixing between denominations can itself be a way of deconstructing negative stereotypes and encouraging genuine relationships between people of different backgrounds. But secondly, the elements of faith which *are* held in common can forge a natural sense of collegiality between churches, which is a potent resource for tackling shared challenges. In other words, in addition to fostering opportunities to mix, ecumenical engagement can also be particularly effective as a means of capitalising on good will and amplifying existing church responses in the community.

The ecumenical landscape in Middlesbrough is a good example of this process emerging over time, since various participants noted that the ecumenical network had expanded and consolidated in recent years (albeit, as one participant from the voluntary sector suggested, predominantly among "certain types" of churches).[213] Of particular significance, two church leaders in separate Anglican parishes noted that greater ecumenical links had enriched relationships with other community stakeholders such as the council:

> If I'm honest, at least at a parish level [ecumenism] may be a bit patchy [but] what I see happening on a bigger scale in town is trust. That the churches, because they've come together as one, there is one point of connection. So the local authorities don't need to say "well you're the Methodist church, and you're the Baptist church – who am I working with here?" The church has... morphed itself into being seen as one. [214]

> We invited the chief exec of the council [to an ecumenical event] and on the Q&A plenary bit at the end he said, "As a council we really want to work with you as churches but we can't work with 50, 60 different churches. Organise yourselves and then we can work with you." Which of course was music to our ears. [215]

We might expect resentment if any other 60 distinct community groups were asked to organise into a single structure, but among churches this was seen as a positive nudge towards things as they should be: that is, the Church working as a single body of different parts.

So too, there was a practical recognition in churches across our case studies that good communication between churches could prevent doubling-up on initiatives and enabled churches to support one another and the community more effectively:

> We went on a Leaders' Day together with all the leaders of the churches and... wrote a list of all the activities each of the churches were doing. And between us, we had virtually everything covered. So someone was doing an Alzheimer's cafe, someone else was doing an hour-long group someone else was doing mums and toddlers. So within the area, every kind of church activity you could think of was covered by one of the churches, but no one church could cover them all. [216]

However, working together is not always so straightforward and the extent to which churches are really "mono-cultural" (as the first participant claimed above) is of course debatable. While some churches certainly find common endeavour comes naturally, the journey to positive ecumenical relationships across the full range of Christian expressions is usually long and iterative. For example, church leaders in Croydon had felt that the old model of ecumenical working was clunky, and was stagnating agile and effective church-based action in the borough. Therefore, they founded the Croydon Churches Forum, which was intended to create a "lighter-touch" way of working together in the community.[217] This has been a positive step. However, there are still difficulties in getting all the churches involved; like Haringey, Croydon also has an extremely fast-moving church landscape, with many transient congregations meeting informally in third-party spaces or houses, and we were told that of around 300-350 churches estimated to be meeting in the borough only 40 are active in the Forum. [218] To bind together such a broad range of distinct and sometimes difficult to reach groups requires an intensive investment of time. Therefore, identifying individuals who are prepared (and supported by their own congregations) to make it the focus of their ministry is vital:

> I was a church leader, I was paid by my church, but I gave 70% of my time to church unity, and working with the council. Most people don't have the luxury of doing that, and so I think if this is to affect the churches, the churches need to think very seriously about funding posts between them, to liaise with councils and all the rest... With everyone moving and changing, to keep that one firm contact point is absolutely critical. [219]

In addition, a separate forum, Together Croydon Churches, was consequently set up separately from Croydon Churches Forum (although not in opposition to it) to represent the distinctive concerns of "Black led and interested Black majority churches" in the borough – particularly on issues that were disproportionately affecting their own congregations. That said, one positive outworking of this group was the organisation of several prayer walks against youth violence in the area – which were in fact run in partnership with the London Peace Alliance (see above, p. 93), demonstrating how ecumenical links can be instrumental in maximising the potential of the churches' innate assets, thus amplifying the churches' positive voice in the community.

Council-church relationships

Unlike ecumenical and interfaith work, where engagement between parties brings its own social cohesion reward, the primary advantages of strong working relationships between churches and councils are pragmatic ones: that church-based assets can be more effectively deployed within the community, and churches can be aware of (and included in) wider strategic plans for the area as they pertain to social cohesion.

Positive engagement between churches and councils varies hugely between areas; while some councils were described as "open and willing", church-based participants in other areas told us they felt "invisible" or viewed with "suspicion".[220] Similarly, while many churches have good working relationships with key community stakeholders, others operate in the community without ever approaching others to collaborate. Positive relationships can rest significantly on the openness of individuals, and various faith-based participants told us that they would approach council officers they knew were sympathetic to faith, just as council-based participants identified individuals that they trusted within faith communities.[221]

Across local authorities, there was an awareness of the need for greater engagement with the faith sector, but this was mainly in the context of constraints on public spending. As these council-based participants, each from a different local authority, acknowledged in their discussion of church-council relations:

> A lot of people still believe local authorities are just going to carry on providing services in the way that we're going to be able to solve everything. And we can't ... I think probably some councils are now hitting the point where they're not viable anymore... We're going to have to get into communities... [and] help communities do more for themselves. [222]

[Churches] are embracing their responsibility to support community, not to [evangelise] everybody... in some cases it's about them filling a gaping hole in services. [223]

Because the reach of the council is declining, because of lack of funds, we will absolutely look for any partners who could help tackle the same issues... Because we want to help to tackle social isolation, we want to help the most vulnerable. We can't do that in as formal way now because we don't have the resources. The church has the same ambition of tackling poverty, tackling homelessness... [224]

The council finds itself in territory that it frankly hasn't been used to really in the past. The last time we had a spike in youth violence was 2006-7. The response was very much from government - there was a big central government programme; as a local authority we responded to that. The context now is very different, so there's a huge onus on how we as the council can play a leadership role in terms of galvanising community action. That's something that the council, frankly, is not particularly used to. [225]

Where in previous years we'd be able to put on events, help coordinate, fund the community groups, give grants out, do a lot of this community capacity building, all of that fell by the wayside over the last probably nine to ten years. So, we're reliant on people coming out from the community wanting change. [226]

These quotations reflect the fact that the majority of church-council interaction pertains to the role of churches in service delivery – which of course has its own indirect

> **66**
> ────────────────
> While some councils were described as "open and willing", church-based participants in other areas told us they felt "invisible" or viewed with "suspicion".

cohesion impact, particularly as it works to keep those who are struggling or on the margins engaged in wider society. In this sense, while the faith sector has significantly diversified over recent decades, and Christianity is no longer included at the decision-making table by default, it is felt on the ground that they have earned their right to be included and heard in these spaces – to the benefit of the community.

However, churches are less often recognised as go-to stakeholders in discussions explicitly pertaining to social cohesion: we heard several church-based participants complain that they had not been included in events and discussions about local cohesion, even though they were active in this area and wanted to contribute. [227] The previous chapter demonstrated the huge amount that churches have to bring to cohesion initiatives – and involving them in planning conversations means bringing all the assets explored in the previous chapter to the table (that is, in many cases the same assets which are so effective of means of delivering public goods). Churches do more than just plug a financial gap, and a senior policy advisor for one of our local authorities reflected:

> *Churches are really, really, really good at what they do in terms of trust and credibility. And I think councils suffer from that, because of the nature of what we do. You know, if we miss a bin we're suddenly the worst council in the world. The thing that councils have is we deliver services to people who don't request them. We also deliver services to people who don't realize that we're delivering services to them... I think what churches, therefore are able to do in partnership with us, is provide almost a friendly face of the city... I think there's a real opportunity for churches to fill that credibility gap.* [228]

It should be noted that trust in religious leaders themselves is not especially high (and has decreased in recent years, not least in the wake of successive child sexual abuse scandals embroiling Christian clergy). The *Ipsos MORI Veracity Index*, which tracks trust in various groups over time, found in 2019 that 64% would generally trust clergy or priests to tell them the truth – down 21 percentage points since 1983, and compared to 95% for the most trusted group (nurses), 76% for the police, 65% for civil servants, 41% for local councillors, and 65% for the ordinary man/woman in the street. [229]

On the other hand, churches are not only their leaders: their embeddedness in communities means that the public face of the local congregation may well be a Christian nurse who volunteers, rather than the ordained church leader.

All that said, not everybody welcomes closer working between councils and churches. As is well-documented elsewhere, concerns around proselytism continue to cast a shadow over churches' work in the community. [230]

So too, some perceive a conflict between local authorities' responsibility to provide services without discrimination on the one hand, and faith and belief groups' (including churches) exemption from some elements of equalities legislation on the other. [231]

However, the exemption itself is narrowly drawn, and makes provision for public service delivery. Thus, under the Equality Act 2010, churches are allowed to discriminate on grounds of religion and belief or sexual orientation (for example, restricting use of their services or facilities) if it is necessary for complying with their organisational purpose, or to avoid conflict with the beliefs of a significant number of their members. However, they are not allowed to discriminate on the grounds of a person's sexual orientation when providing services on behalf of a public authority.[232]

This does mean they could restrict services by religious affiliation while receiving public funds in some circumstances, but there are situations in which this might be appropriate and beneficial to cohesion; for example, attendance at a council-funded ecumenical forum might be restricted to Christians, but only because this relates to its organisational purpose – and it would not be able to discriminate on other grounds.[233]

That said, nervousness around equalities legislation can mean that public authorities are happier to support initiatives framed as "cultural" rather than "religious". This perhaps reflects an assumption that "culture" can be about behaviours which do not preclude a shared common worldview, while it is feared that religion may involve beliefs and ideas that clash with "British values" as defined by the state. As previous Theos work has argued, such "progressive tests" are themselves divisive for cohesion, implying there is only room for one set of values in our public life – which of course demonstrably undermines any notion of social cohesion that claims to prize working together across differences – and narrowing the range of community groups which are able to contribute. Instead, public authorities should employ "relational tests" in which organisations should be asked to demonstrate their willingness to work across different backgrounds and perspectives.[234]

After all, there are many ways of ensuring that both parties are clear of their basic responsibilities (including those according to equalities legislation) without making loaded judgement calls – for example, the Faith Covenant established by the All-Party Parliamentary Group on Faith and Society, which offers a blueprint for best practice expectations on both faith groups and local authorities in partnership work.[235] Open conversations around these issues can even be a positive prompt within churches, for example by encouraging them to include more female and younger voices in their public representation (a commonly noted limitation of public faith leadership, as noted above).[236]

So too, while of course some churches view service delivery as an opportunity to proselytise, these instances are rare. Others do not think the two should mix at all, and most (somewhere in between the two extremes) have a well-developed conception of how the relationship between evangelism and service provision might be navigated appropriately. For example:

> *Our number one driving force is we want to transform people's lives spiritually. You know, we want to see them coming to a personal relationship with Christ, and that will always be our primary focus. However, if a person doesn't make that commitment, but we can help them economically, if we can help them become debt free, if we can help them with their housing situation and things like that, that's still part of us being the salt and light of Christ in our community. So we don't want to be mercenary... Our heart is just to bless the community. So I guess I probably should have started with our vision statement. Our vision statement is "A light on a hill, transforming our community one person at a time."*[237]

It is also increasingly common for churches to establish separate charities through which their social outreach or community engagement is coordinated, either to establish a critical distance between church and service, or to avoid negative perceptions of Christianity adversely affecting their capacity to contribute.[238] Churches therefore should not be dismissed out of hand, and are usually ready and eager to have conversations with potential partners about how they might serve the community effectively and sensitively, but also authentically.

After all, underlying all these concerns are more fundamental questions: what actually is a church, and why should churches engage with their communities at all? Of course, as explored above, churches must uphold shared public standards around safeguarding and financial accountability. However, they are not, in essence, service providers – and something is certainly lost when councils only value churches and faith groups insofar as they are willing to take on this role:

> *The challenge for us is we don't want to be just a social service. Because the reason we're doing it is because we're trying to introduce people to the love of God... It's not like we're trying to proselytise here... All we're trying to do is tell people that God loves them. That really God loves them. But if we're not allowed to say that, then we begin to feel like we're just being an unpaid for government agency.*[239]

By the same measure, it is not always appropriate for churches to do exactly what a public service might – as churches themselves are keen to admit. For example, we heard church-based participants reflecting that they would not feel comfortable taking on a law enforcement role, or denying help to those without recourse to public funds.[240] In both senses they fundamentally differ in outlook and purpose from local authorities.

Nor are the churches' assets necessarily being wasted if they are not directed towards the delivery of public services. Of course, it is always a positive thing where church resources are used to help the community; it is a Christian injunction to love one's neighbour, and there is unfulfilled potential among many churches which often stems from a lack of vision on the church's part. However, churches may legitimately feel led to express their spiritual calling in a less public way – and this is not necessarily without a cohesion benefit. For example, considering the conversion of half an Anglican church into a soft play area for local children, we heard one local councillor querying, "Why not deconsecrate [the whole building] and turn it into a completely you know, a leisure facility?"[241] In this case, meeting the spiritual needs of the congregation was not immediately recognised as an act of service to the community in its own right. Yet, as has been noted above, worship can itself foster both bridging and bonding capital, as well as promoting feelings of confidence and dignity within individuals. More fundamentally, it is the engine of the church, fulfilling the basic spiritual needs of those who attend – without which there would be no congregation, and no soft play area at all.

> Churches must uphold shared public standards around safeguarding and financial accountability. However, they are not, in essence, service providers.

In short, as one church leader working on a deprived Plymouth estate memorably reflected, "there is a difference between putting on services and serving people". This distinction – between serving and services – is a critical and helpful one in understanding the motivations of church-based social involvement. Considering the relationship between his church, the community hub focused around the local café, and the funding brought into the estate through the Big Local, he further explained, "My role is to serve them in what they're doing, and for them to be the best expression of God's grace as they can".[242] In this way, each organisation has a different role in the community – and where the appropriate roles and assets of each are recognised on their own terms, it can unleash the power of the churches' assets for greater service to the community. Conversely, the community is likely to miss out where these different roles and assets are collapsed into one.

A positive example of this dynamic can again be found in Bolton, and especially in the enthusiasm with which churches have embraced and promoted the Bolton 2030 Vision – a strategic vision for Bolton's future as a town, led by a partnership of various key local stakeholders, including the council, community leaders, faith leaders, police, healthcare and educational professionals. Bolton Christian Community Cohesion (a collective of local Christian organisations) is part of the partnership, and hosted three 'Passion for the Bolton 2030 Vision' conferences throughout 2018 as well as producing the 'We Support Bolton 2030 Vision' plaques that are displayed at many churches and other organisations across the town. In response to the trust that has been placed in churches, they demonstrably feel ownership for – and actively celebrate – their town's strategy.[243] In this way a healthy relationship where faith is mobilised according to its natural strengths, rather than viewed with suspicion, has led to the Vision having much wider impact and buy-in than it otherwise might have done.

Conclusion

Strong working relationships (and even, in some cases, official partnerships) between churches and other community stakeholders can unleash significant positive energy in pursuit of more cohesive societies. Where different faiths are able to engage positively, negative stereotypes are broken down, and additional energy is released to tackle shared problems together; between churches, investing in a natural sense of collegiality can often form the basis of a more coordinated and concerted approach to Christian community engagement; and between churches and councils, strong working relationships drive forward local empowerment in a way that neither party could achieve alone.

Crucially, the exact nature and potential of these relationships (as well as the problems which can undermine them) are different in each of the three examples explored above. This underlines the specificity of churches as they work in the community – that is, the ways in which churches differ from other community organisations – and relationships work most effectively where their distinctive nature is embraced, rather than treated with suspicion or frustration. Above all, a recognition that churches' religious motivation is definitive of their community contribution, so cannot simply be stripped away or ignored (and related to this, an acceptance that there is space for a range of values and worldviews in a fully cohesive and open society) should form the basis of these positive working relationships as local authorities. This will only become more important as the state increasingly relies on the church contribution to meet the needs of communities across the country.

[198] Church #274.

[199] Church #213.

[200] L. Casey, *The Casey Review*, p. 149; J. Fahy and J. Bock, *Beyond Dialogue? Interfaith Engagement in Delhi, Doha and London* (Cambridge: The Woolf Institute, 2018), p. 10-11.

[201] The Inter Faith Network for the United Kingdom, *The changing face of local interfaith dialogue and cooperation* (London: IFN, 2020), p. 5-6. www.interfaith.org.uk/uploads/IFN_2019_National_Meeting_Report_%28Hi%29.pdf

[202] Non-church #144.

[203] For example, Church #60, Church #109, Church #277, Church #354, Non-church #15, Church #20, Church #299, Church #149.

[204] Pennington, *Cohesive Societies*, p. 41.

[205] Non-church #10.

[206] Faith in Newham, *Introduction*,. faithinnewham.co.uk/

[207] Emmanuel Ministries, Forest Gate Emmanuel Church, *Faithful Friends*,. forestgate-emmanuel-church.com/page/318/ministry-faithful-friends-page

[208] Non-church #87, Church #91, Non-church #94.

[209] Church #190.

[210] Non-church #144.

[211] Non-church #74.

[212] Church #108.

[213] Church #38, Non-church #45, Church #48, Church #54, Church #55.

[214] Church #38.

[215] Church #48.

[216] Church #183.

[217] Church #133.

[218] Church #136.

[219] Church #133.

[220] Church #26, Church #161, Church #331.

[221] Church #283, Non-church #264, Non-church #111.

[222] Non-church #200.

[223] Non-church #1.

[224] Non-church #157.

[225] Non-church #119.

[226] Non-church #228.

[227] Church #195, Church #108, Church #216.

[228] Non-church #174.

[229] Ipsos MORI, *Ipsos MORI Veracity Index 2019: Trust in Professions survey*, (London: Ipsos MORI, 2019) www.ipsos.com/sites/default/files/ct/news/documents/2019-11/trust-in-professions-veracity-index-2019-slides.pdf

[230] S. Hilhorst and D. Barclay, *Holy Alliances: Church-Secular Partnerships for Social Good* (London: Demos, 2019), p. 12-13, demos.co.uk/wp-content/uploads/2019/09/Holy-Alliances-digital-final-.pdf; P. Bickley, *The Problem of Proselytism* (London: Theos, 2015). www.theosthinktank.co.uk/cmsfiles/archive/files/Problem%20of%20Proselytism%20web%20version.pdf

[231] British Humanist Association, *Quality and Equality: Human Rights, Public Services and Religious Organisations* (London: BHA, 2007), p.14-15, humanism.org.uk/wp-content/uploads/BHA-Public-Services-Report-Quality-and-Equality.pdf

[232] It is also worth noting that this exemption applies only to organisations whose organisational purpose is a religious one and does not apply in commercial settings. See Equality Act 2010 Schedule 23 para 2 (10), www.legislation.gov.uk/ukpga/2010/15/schedule/23

[233] Equality and Human Rights Commission, *Religion or belief: is the law working?* (Manchester: EHRC, 2016), p. 41-42, 47.

[234] D. Barclay, *Making multiculturalism work: enabling practical action across deep difference* (London: Theos, 2013), p. 9, 29-30. www.theosthinktank.co.uk/cmsfiles/archive/files/Reports/Making%20Multiculturalism%20Work%20combined.pdf

[235] APPG Faith and Society, *Faith Covenant in Full*, , www.faithandsociety.org/covenant/full/

[236] Non-church #246.

[237] Church #18.

[238] Church #73, Church #54, Church #214, Church #338.

[239] Church #108.

[240] Church #129, Church #336, Church #340, Church #187, Church #57.

[241] Non-church #318.

[242] Church #188.

[243] Church #13, Church #28, Church #20, Church #11, Church #16, Church #18.

Conclusion and Recommendations

Social cohesion – which we have understood to refer to the strength of our collective relationships – is vital for any society to meet shared challenges, commemorate shared achievements, and build a common life together. In policy terms, "community cohesion" was forged as a distinct policy area in the wake of "race riots" affecting towns across Northern England, and much of consequent cohesion policy has similarly been driven forward in response to crisis. This has led to a focus on religion as a risk factor for division, and there has been a neglect of consideration for how churches operate in their communities (positively or negatively) on an ongoing basis as a distinct part of civil society. The Free Churches Commission has drawn on the insights of nearly 400 people across fourteen English local authorities to consider this contribution in greater detail. Our conclusions are broadly threefold, and give rise to a series of recommendations for both churches and those hoping to engage better with them in pursuit of a more cohesive society. A fuller practical reflection can be found in the two How-To booklets that have been published alongside this report.[244]

> Working with churches can form part of the necessary move beyond a crisis-driven approach.

First, at their best, churches are emblematic of an approach that views cohesion as a desirable outcome in its own right.

This is in contrast to cohesion policy, which has usually been driven forward by instances where cohesion has already broken down. **Policymakers should ensure that they are working with churches wherever possible and appropriate as a practical step towards a less crisis-driven approach**

to cohesion issues. After all, far greater focus is needed on precisely these elements of cohesion which affect us all as we move towards a wider and more holistic understanding of cohesive societies – not merely as those societies which are not (yet) falling apart, but as those in which people of different ethnicities, socio-economic groups, ages, or simply those we just don't know personally, work together towards the common good. Churches are often working in precisely this manner to make a positive cohesion impact behind the scenes and below the radar – and they have their own, authentically Christian reasons to care about social cohesion as an end in itself. Indeed, Theos researchers were struck by just how often church-based responses were imbued with a theological understanding of cohesion and the need to engage with one's community – that is, to be salt and light to the world, to build the kingdom of God on earth, to care for one's town or city, and to love one's neighbour.

> Churches should ensure their community engagement takes into account what the community needs, what is already happening, and what the congregation will support.

So too, given this religious impetus to serve, churches are often (though not always) deeply embedded in their local communities – and most successfully serve their neighbourhoods where they capitalise on this natural strength. **Where churches themselves want to start something new, they should therefore first consider what is already going on in the neighbourhood, what the community needs, and what the congregation will support.** In other words, their engagement should be tailored to the community in which the church sits.

This approach is equally available to all churches – not only those which officially operate according to a parochial model – although the parish system is a good example of a strong practical framework which promotes engagement on precisely this basis.

66

Churches should systematically reflect on their assets and how they can maximise their use of them.

Alongside an understanding of community need, churches also bring a range of their own valuable assets to the community, and where they have a realistic understanding of these resources, their impact on social cohesion can be transformative. Not only do they offer an unrivalled source of physical capital scattered equally throughout the country; so too, they act as the social capillaries of their communities, offering a wellspring of natural and formal leadership, convening difficult conversations between different groups, motivating individual members of their congregations to give back, and seeing (and enacting) the full potential of their communities where others do not. Therefore, **churches hoping to maximise their social cohesion impact should systematically reflect on their available assets, and consider ways in which these existing resources can be used more effectively.** For example, are "bump moments" between rental groups being maximised? Are rental prices affordable for local and grassroots, or charity groups? Do congregations feel empowered to take on leadership roles? Are maintenance concerns a distraction or a burden? What can be done to release the natural assets of the church into service, and make churches more accessible to individuals in the community?

Secondly, on many of these points, churches illustrate the limitations of any approach that views only bridging capital as a route to a more cohesive society.

There are many instances where bonding capital along one measure can generate bridging capital along a range of others. So too, bonding capital itself can be highly positive as a way of promoting feelings of belonging and confidence, and indeed, of enabling a range of people from different backgrounds to feel equal ownership over the public sphere. A truly cohesive society is not one in which everybody agrees, but one in which everyone feels they have a stake – and this equally requires bridging and bonding opportunities. In this sense, this report has offered a practical elaboration on the conceptual conclusions of the *Cohesive Societies: Faith and Belief* review published earlier this year: **those working on cohesion issues should be prepared to engage with, and promote, both bridging and bonding opportunities as they emerge practically in local communities and beyond.**[245]

> All cohesion stakeholders should be prepared to engage with, and promote, both bridging and bonding opportunities in local communities and beyond.

Working with churches is one concrete way in which they can do this.

That said, there is a clear difference between promoting positive bonding capital and bolstering existing inequalities, or entrenching inward-looking communities. Especially where churches have a clearly delineated responsibility to serve the wider community, whether through church-run schools or the provision of council-funded community services, they should **take special care to promote inclusion and**

diversity in their spaces; this includes mitigating against any negative impact of faith-based school admissions on existing inequalities. As for the church context itself, nurturing congregational life is important, but churches leave their own potential unfulfilled when they become too concerned with maintenance of their own communities – and especially where they equate the good of their communities with the good of their own buildings. Naturally, looking beyond one's own congregation enhances one's positive impact on social cohesion. This is not an either-or choice, but can inspire the wider community to care for the church in return; nor is it a neglect of the Church's mission, but a fulfilment of it.

> Churches should take special care to promote inclusion and diversity in their spaces, including church-run schools.

Thirdly, churches are not just generic community groups, and their full potential is realised only where the distinctive features that come with a religious motivation are recognised.

Not only do churches have their own authentic motivations for engaging in the community (chapter one), and a particular pattern of assets which characterises their nature as churches (chapter two), but the way they engage with others is marked by their authentic nature as churches (chapter three). Therefore, what makes positive interfaith engagement is not necessarily the same as what makes positive ecumenical work, or a positive relationship between church and council. There is room for all these relationships in a truly cohesive society, in all their diversity and specificity – and cohesion is served best when each party is recognised for what it can uniquely offer. Therefore, those working on cohesion policy and strategy – whether local authorities, charities, police, healthcare professionals, other faith groups, or even churches themselves – should **take account of the specific ways in which churches operate in their communities,** and include them at the decision-making table on this basis rather than expecting everyone to engage in the same way.

On all these points, the churches' care for their communities reflect a practical outworking of their Christian faith, and especially the Christian injunction to love one's neighbour as oneself. A society which embraces the role of churches as key stakeholders in cohesion discussions on this basis will be a more rounded one, more comfortable with difference, and more confident in its underlying unity. That is to say, it will be a more cohesive community – both at a local level and beyond:

Cohesion stakeholders should take account of the specific ways churches engage, rather than assuming they are generic aspects of the faith or community sectors.

> *I think probably social cohesion is loving your neighbour as yourself. That's what I think social cohesion is. That neighbour is a global neighbour, it's a local neighbour, it's a neighbour who you hate, and it's a neighbour who you don't know, but it is all about neighbour. Social cohesion is a place that... is realistic and also inclusive. So, it sees what its assets are and it offers them to each other, and when it can't, it recognises that it can't and it turns to its good neighbour and it says, "Can you?"* [246]

244 M. Pennington, *Nurturing Social Cohesion: Why it matters and what your church can do about it* (London: Theos, 2020); M. Pennington, *Nurturing Social Cohesion: A how-to guide for engaging churches* (London: Theos, 2020).

245 Pennington, *Cohesive Societies*, p. 62.

246 Church #332.

Appendix

Appendix: Case Study Areas

Theos researchers visited fourteen local authorities across England between November 2018 and September 2019. The case study areas were chosen to reflect a range of potential cohesion challenges, and to maintain a balance across all nine administrative regions of England. It is worth noting that not all of these areas were chosen on the basis of economic deprivation; on the contrary, some were notably affluent, so avoiding any assumption that economic deprivation necessitates poor cohesion outcomes. A short summary of each is listed below.

Bolton is a large town in the north west of England and was a hub of the textile industry until the mid-twentieth century, when it moved to a service-based economy. 18.1% of children in the local authority are now being raised in out of work households,[247] and Bolton had the sixth highest proportion of empty shops in the country in 2017.[248] The town also has a large refugee community, having been made a dispersal area in the government's Resettlement Scheme in 2001.

Bradford is a large city in West Yorkshire and one of two government Integration Areas in our sample (along with Peterborough). Bradford is highly ethnically diverse: according to the most recent census data, 17.2% of its population was born outside the UK (compared to an England average of 13.8%) and 63.9% identify as White British (compared to an England average of 79.8%). It is also religiously diverse: the largest religious group is still Christian, but the proportion of Christian respondents fell from 60.1% to 45.9% between the 2001 and 2011 censuses. Nearly one quarter of Bradford's population identified themselves as Muslim in 2011 – an increase of 8%

to 24.7% since 2001 – and the area had fewer non-religious respondents than the national or regional averages. [249]

Bury is a town in the north west of England, whose local authority boundaries extend down to the northern edge of Manchester. As of the 2011 census, the local authority was home to the second largest Jewish community outside London; this population is largely concentrated in the areas of Prestwich and Whitefield, and these areas formed the focus of our visit.[250] Prestwich in particular is an up-and-coming area to live, increasingly popular with young professionals working in Manchester.

Cornwall is the first of two rural local authorities in our study, and contains the most deprived areas in the whole country by European standards; the region is also the least economically productive in the UK, though its productivity has been increasing.[251] Its traditional industries are fishing, farming, and clay mining, but the mining and fishing industries have faced substantial decline, albeit alongside a growth in tourism. The rise of second home ownership is particularly contentious in Cornwall: over 1 in 10 homes in Cornwall do not have a usual resident, and in the five parishes of Cornwall where second homes account for more than 35% of all housing, the average house price is 87% above the Cornwall average.[252] We focused our visit on two rural areas which were notably deprived according to *the 2015 Index of Multiple Deprivation*: the clay mining villages situated to the north of St Austell, and the rural areas surrounding Penzance. [253]

Croydon is a south London borough which is easily commutable to central London. It has its own large commercial centre and is slowly gentrifying, though its regeneration has been somewhat overshadowed by uncertainty over whether a new Westfield shopping centre will be built there.[254]

The borough has also struggled with knife and violent crime (and a reputation for the same), though this has reduced in recent years and is now below the London average.[255]

The Home Office is based in Croydon, meaning all asylum seekers coming into the UK pass through the borough at some point in their settlement process.

Derby is a city in the East Midlands. It was the fourth least equal local authority in England measured by the standard deviation of the mean *Index of Multiple Deprivation* score of its LSOAs (Lower Standard Output Areas).[256]

It has a significant ethnic minority population, largely clustered in the south-west parts of the city, and especially in Arboretum and Normanton wards.[257]

It is also home to various advanced manufacturing companies, including Rolls Royce and Bombardia (though in the wake of the coronavirus pandemic, Rolls Royce announced in May 2020 that it was cutting a devastating 9,000 jobs across the company, including 1,500 in Derby and Nottinghamshire).[258]

East Lindsey is the second of two rural local authorities in our study, stretching from east of Lincoln to the coast. It is a popular retirement destination, particularly around the coastal areas where 28.2% of residents are over 65 (compared to 16.3% in England as a whole). At the same time, it has high youth unemployment, above average levels of children in poverty, and 33% of residents have no qualifications. It was one of ten local authorities with the largest percentage point increase between the *2010 and 2015 Indices of Multiple Deprivation* (IMD), and its average IMD score was 30th most deprived of all English local authorities in 2019; it is very unusual to have this level of deprivation in a rural area.[259]

Haringey is a north London borough in which over 1 in 3 children live in poverty after housing costs, though the borough also contains notably affluent neighbourhoods such as Muswell Hill.[260] The borough has the highest rate of knife crime with injury in London.[261] The 2011 August riots began in Haringey, after Mark Duggan was shot dead by police in the borough; the independent Riots, Communities and Victims Panel found that 71% of these riots occurred within the 10% of areas of the country ranked as the least socially cohesive. [262]

Middlesbrough is a town in the north east of England which, as a local authority, had the highest proportion of LSOAs in the 10% most deprived according to the *2019 Index of Multiple Deprivation*.[263] In 2015, Middlesbrough was also found to be the only place in the country where more than one in 200 of the local population was a refugee or asylum seeker (the recommended limit in government guidance).[264] Its traditional industry is steelwork, but that industry has dramatically reduced in recent years.[265]

Newham was the home of the London 2012 Olympics and has unsurprisingly experienced significant regeneration in the past decade – but this investment has been spread unevenly. Between 2005 and 2015, Newham's population grew from 258,000 to 334,000, and the borough had the highest growth in the non-UK born population in London between the 2001 and 2011 census. [266]

Peterborough is a city in the East Midlands, and one of two government Integration Areas in our sample, along with Bradford. In marked contrast to many of our post-industrial case studies, Peterborough has seen rapid population growth over recent decades, amounting to a 148.2% increase in its non-UK born population between 2001 and 2011.[267]

More than half the city's total population are now immigrants, and its rapid growth has been compounded by its status as a commuter city for London, as well as a boom in local industry.

Plymouth is a city in the south west of England. Some of its large suburban neighbourhoods were only incorporated into the city in 1967, and its constituent areas differ dramatically: it was strikingly reported in July 2019 that one seven-mile bus journey across Plymouth saw the life expectancy reduce by up to a year at each stop, and by seven years in total.[268] Plymouth has the second highest level of personal debt in England and Wales.[269] Historically, Plymouth has been unusually ethnically homogenous: 96.2% of the population identified as White, and 92.9% as White British, in the 2011 census, and the largest single minority ethnic group was Chinese at 0.5%. However, greater diversity is likely to be reflected in the upcoming census, as Plymouth's ethnic minority population has grown rapidly in recent years.[270]

Solihull is an affluent town in the West Midlands, and was notably identified by uSwitch as the "best place to live" in the UK in 2013 (though it has since dropped in the rankings).[271] However, its local authority boundaries extend far beyond the town itself to the eastern edge of Birmingham, and encompass some of the most deprived communities in the country.[272] Solihull is consequently the least equal local authority in

England, measured by the standard deviation of the mean *2015 Index of Multiple Deprivation* score of its LSOAs. [273]

Thanet is a district in east Kent, whose main settlements are Margate, Ramsgate and Broadstairs. UKIP won control of Thanet District Council during the 2015 election – the party's only local authority in the country to date – but this support has since waned: partly due to internal divisions within the local party, UKIP lost all its councillors in Thanet in 2018.[274]

Thanet is the second most deprived local authority in south east England, and the thirty-seventh most deprived in the country, judged by the proportion of its LSOAs in the most 10% deprived nationally.[275]

We found that the district's relationship with London was a particular source of local contention: not only are many vulnerable adults and children from London-based local authorities placed in Thanet, but many affluent Londoners also leave the city to live permanently in the district – the so-called "DFLS" ("Down from London").

[247] Oxford Consultants for Social Inclusion, *Local Insight: Bolton* (Brighton: OSCI, 2019), p. 19.

[248] D. Holland, 'Bolton town centre is sixth worst in UK for empty shops', *The Bolton News*, 22 March 2017, www.theboltonnews.co.uk/news/15172691. bolton-town-centre-is-sixth-worst-in-uk-for-empty-shops/

[249] Bradford Metropolitan District Council, *2011 Census Release 2.1: Key Statistics for Local Authorities, Bradford Release* (Bradford: City of Bradford Metropolitan District Council,2011), ubd.bradford.gov.uk/ media/1275/2011-census-second-release-11-december-summary-note.pdf

[250] Institute for Jewish Policy Research, *Largest Jewish Populations in the United Kingdom in 2011 by Local Authority* (London: Institute for Jewish Policy Research, 2011) jpr.org.uk/documents/Largest_Jewish_ populations_by_Local_Authority.2001_and_2011_comparison.pdf

[251] C. Campos and A. Patel, *Subregional productivity in the UK* (London: *Office for National Statistics*, 2020) www.ons.gov.uk/ employmentandlabourmarket/peopleinwork/labourproductivity/ articles/regionalandsubregionalproductivityintheuk/ february2020#results-for-nuts2-subregions

[252] Cornwall Local Plan, *Second and Holiday Homes: Housing Evidence Base Briefing Note 11*, (2015), www.cornwallhousing.org.uk/ media/17171641/bn11-second-and-holiday-homes-v2-dec-15.pdf

[253] ArcGIS, *Index of Multiple Deprivation 2015*, (Redlands, CA.: Enviromental Systems Research Institute, 2015), www.arcgis.com/home/webmap/ viewer.html?webmap=14b9617e617c4ae09c0a5b0cab06044b

[254] See, for example, *Inside Croydon*, 'Labour councillors signal major Town Hall U-turn over Westfield', Inside Croydon, 19 June 2020, insidecroydon.com/2020/06/19/labour-councillors- signal-major-town-hall-u-turn-over-westfield/

[255] Strategic Partnership Croydon, *Borough Profile: December 2018* (Croydon: Croydon Council, 2018) www.croydonobservatory.org/ wp-content/uploads/2019/01/BOROUGH-PROFILE_DEC2018.pdf

[256] J. Bradshaw and K. Bloor, *Which Local Authorities are Most Unequal?*, (York: University of York, 2016), p. 3-4. pure.york.ac.uk/portal/en/publications/which- local-authorities-are-most-unequal(eba28517-2c13-4bf9-b8d0-e71a13201340).html

(Note, an LSOA is a small geographical unit of between 1000 and 3000 people.)

[257] Compare, for example:

UK census data, *Allestree* (ONS), www.ukcensusdata.com/ allestree-e05001768#sthash.YVeeU9KJ.O3UPzZ2v.dpbs;

UK census data, *Arboretum* (ONS), www.ukcensusdata.com/ arboretum-e05001770#sthash.fQAgJBds.dpbs

UK census data, *Normanton* (ONS), www.ukcensusdata.com/
normanton-e05001780#sthash.84V3e8I5.dpbs

258 T. Bokros, 'Rolls Royce reveals exact number of job losses in Derby
and Nottinghamshire', *Derby Telegraph*, 3 June 2020, www.derbytelegraph.
co.uk/news/derby-news/rolls-royce-reveals-exact-number-4190102

259 East Lindsey District Council, *East Lindsey Economic Baseline 2016*, (East
Lindsey: East Lindsey District Council, 2016)www.e-lindsey.gov.uk/
media/5128/Economic-Baseline-2016-Key-Messages-Voluntary-Community/
pdf/Economic_Baseline_2016__Key_Messages_-_Voluntary__Community.
pdf ; Ministry of Housing, Communities & Local Government, English indices
of deprivation 2019: File 10: Local authority district summaries, (London:
Ministry of Housing, Communities and Local Government, 2019) https://
www.gov.uk/government/statistics/english-indices-of-deprivation-2019

260 Child Poverty Action Group, *Child Poverty in London Facts* (London:
Child Poverty Action Group) cpag.org.uk/child-poverty-london-facts

261 Haringey Council, *Haringey at a Glance: State of the Borough* (Haringey:
Haringey Council, 2020) www.haringey.gov.uk/sites/haringeygovuk/
files/state_of_the_borough_final_master_version.pdf

262 D. Singh, *Five Days in August: An interim report on the 2011 English
riots* (Riots Communities and Victims Panel, 2011), p. 62.

263 Ministry of Housing, Communities and Local Government, *The English
Indices of Deprivation 2019* (London: Ministry of Housing, Communities and Local
Government, 2019), p. 11. assets.publishing.service.gov.uk/government/uploads/
system/uploads/attachment_data/file/835115/IoD2019_Statistical_Release.pdf

264 J. Reed, 'Why Does Middlesbrough Have the Most Asylum Seekers?',
BBC News, 23 October 2015, www.bbc.co.uk/news/uk-34597022

265 BBC News, 'A History of Teesside Steelmaking', *BBC News*, 23 November
2010. news.bbc.co.uk/local/tees/hi/people_and_places/history/
newsid_9220000/9220056.stm#:~:text=Teesside's%20steel%20industry%20
was%20born,employed%20more%20than%2040%2C000%20people

266 London Councils, *Promoting successful social integration
in London* (London: London Councils, 2017), p. 49.

267 Cambridgeshire County Council and Cambridgeshire and Peterborough
Clinical Commissioning Group, *Migrant and Refugee Joint Strategic Needs
Assessment for Cambridgeshire, 2016* (2016), p. 8. cambridgeshireinsight.org.uk/
wp-content/uploads/2018/09/Cambs-Migrant-JSNA-full-v12_0-FINAL.pdf

268 C. Smith, 'The Plymouth Bus Journey Where Life Expectancy Gets Worse
at Every Stop', *Plymouth Herald*, 15 July 2019, https://www.plymouthherald.
co.uk/news/plymouth-news/plymouth-bus-journey-life-expectancy-3078165

[269] R. Partington, 'Stoke is debt capital of England and Wales – followed by Plymouth', *The Guardian*, 13 July 2018 www.theguardian.com/money/2018/jul/13/stoke-is-debt-capital-of-england-and-wales-followed-by-plymouth

[270] Plymouth Council, *The Plymouth Report* (Plymouth: Public Health, Plymouth City Council, 2014), p. 16. www.plymouth.gov.uk/sites/default/files/PlymouthReport_2014.pdf

[271] H. Saul, 'Ten best places to live in the UK: Solihull comes top', *The Independent*, 14 November 2013, www.independent.co.uk/news/uk/home-news/ten-best-places-to-live-in-the-uk-solihull-comes-top-8938636.html

[272] Solihull Metropolitan Borough Council, *Solihull Metropolitan Borough: A Brief History,*. www.solihull.gov.uk/Resident/Libraries/Local-family-history/solihullboroughhistory ; *Solihull Metropolitan Borough Council, Chelmsley Wood History,*. www.solihull.gov.uk/Resident/Libraries/Local-family-history/localhistory/chelmsleywoodhistory >

[273] J. Bradshaw and K. Bloor, *Which Local Authorities are Most Unequal?*, p. 3-4.

[274] Thanet District Council, *Thanet District Council Election – Thursday, 7 May, 2015*, democracy.thanet.gov.uk/mgElectionResults.aspx?ID=69&RPID=21356845; Thanet District Council, *Thanet District Council Election – Thursday, 2 May, 2019*, democracy.thanet.gov.uk/mgElectionResults.aspx?ID=76&RPID=21356845 >

[275] Ministry of Housing, Communities & Local Government, English indices of deprivation 2019: *File 10....* www.gov.uk/government/statistics/english-indices-of-deprivation-2019

Theos – enriching conversations

Theos exists to enrich the conversation about the role of faith in society.

Religion and faith have become key public issues in this century, nationally and globally. As our society grows more religiously diverse, we must grapple with religion as a significant force in public life. All too often, though, opinions in this area are reactionary or ill informed.

We exist to change this

We want to help people move beyond common misconceptions about faith and religion, behind the headlines and beneath the surface. Our rigorous approach gives us the ability to express informed views with confidence and clarity.

As the UK's leading religion and society think tank, we reach millions of people with our ideas. Through our reports, events and media commentary, we influence today's influencers and decision makers. According to *The Economist*, we're "an organisation that demands attention". We believe Christianity can contribute to the common good and that faith, given space in the public square, will help the UK to flourish.

6

Will you partner with us?

Theos receives no government, corporate or denominational funding. We rely on donations from individuals and organisations to continue our vital work. Please consider signing up as a Theos Friend or Associate or making a one off donation today.

Theos Friends and Students

— Stay up to date with our monthly newsletter

— Receive (free) printed copies of our reports

— Get free tickets to all our events

£7/ month
for Friends

£4/ month
for Students

Theos Associates

— Stay up to date with our monthly newsletter

— Receive (free) printed copies of our reports

— Get free tickets to all our events

— Get invites to private events with the Theos team and other Theos Associates

£32/ month

Sign up on our website:
www.theosthinktank.co.uk/about/support-us